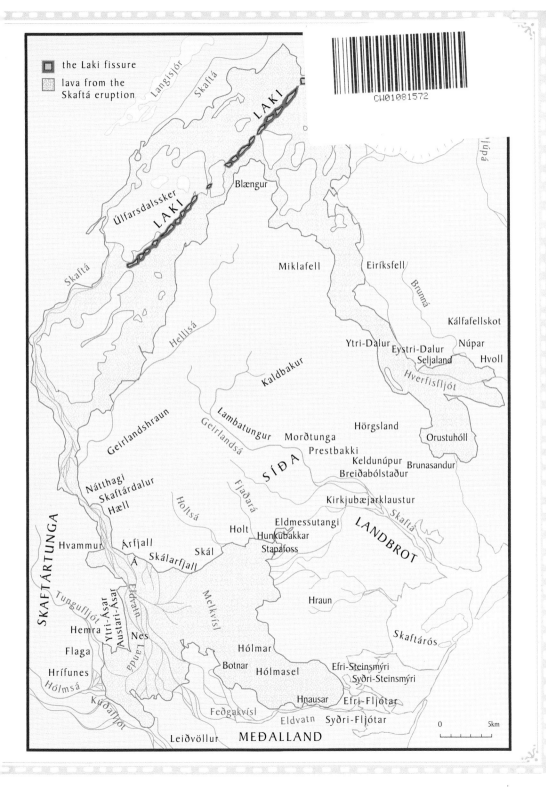

Fires of the Earth

THE LAKI ERUPTION 1783-1784

Fires of the Earth

THE LAKI ERUPTION 1783-1784

by the Rev. Jón Steingrímsson

Introduction by Dr. Guðmundur E. Sigvaldason

English translation by Keneva Kunz

Original title: *Fullkomið rit um Síðueld*
First printed in Iceland 1907
Copyright © 1998 by the University of Iceland Press and the Nordic Volcanological Institute
Translation copyright © 1998 by Keneva Kunz
Editor: Þórgunnur Skúladóttir
Design: Magnús Valur Pálsson
Illustrations: Brian Pilkington
Photos of original manuscript: The National Archive of Iceland

Published by the Nordic Volcanological Institute
and the University of Iceland Press, Reykjavík, Iceland, 1998

Printed in Iceland

ISBN 9979-54-244-6

Introduction

IN THE YEAR 1783 a volcanic eruption broke out in southern Iceland. Before it stopped eight months later it had produced a larger amount of lava than any eruption on record in the world in historical times. News of this enormous natural catastrophe spread slowly to the outside world, much slower than the unhealthy fumes emanating from the molten lava. Carried by wind, the volcanic fumes caused crop failure over large parts of the northern hemisphere and deterioration of climate. In Iceland this volcanic event, commonly called the Laki eruption or eruption from the Laki fissure, became a national calamity. While the eruption and the flowing lava did not cause direct loss of life, their poisonous indirect effects killed a large proportion of the domestic animals. That in turn caused famine and disease which resulted in the death of some ten thousand people.

Nowhere were the noxious effects of the eruption felt stronger than in the very district where the lava belched forth with its great force and in enormous quantities. History shows that when man is faced with overwhelming odds, everything may depend on the existence of a person who is able and willing to assume leadership in an apparently hopeless battle. In the "district of fire", as the Síða district was sometimes called, that leadership was found in pastor Jón Steingrímsson who served the church at Kirkjubæjarklaustur. His performance during and after the eruption has made him a legendary figure in the minds of Icelanders, amplified by the common belief that he performed the miracle of stopping the lava when it approached his parish. His own interpretation of that particular event is given to us in this book, along with an account of the eruption and its effects, in such detail and clarity as to make it a scientific classic as well as a literary jewel.

Born in 1728, Jón Steingrímsson was 50 years old when he assumed his ministry in the Síða district, where he served for the rest of his life. His account of the eruption is only a small example of his literary activities. His major work is an autobiography, one of the most significant and interesting lives ever written in Icelandic. With great frankness and at times nearly naive openness this book describes an energetic and versatile man who displayed his great mental strength, faith in God and sense of duty when such qualities were most urgently required, during the "Fire".

The present book, with the original title "A Complete Treatise on the Síða Fires", is the first full-length work to be published in a foreign language. References to the manuscript had already reached the outside scientific world in the years following the events, and short passages have been translated and published in connection with later scientific studies on this major eruption. In 1783 the only description of a lava flow that existed in scientific literature was from the 1669 eruption of Etna, a lava flow with a volume ten times less than the Laki lava. Other descriptions were mainly concerned with explosive eruptions but in general systematic knowledge and understanding of volcanic phenomena was at a very early stage.

The little that was known outside Iceland about Jón Steingrímsson's observations did have some effect on scientific thought at the time. We will never know, however, what impact they might have had on the development of volcanology if his text had been written in a language known to more people than the 30,000 Icelanders who survived the calamities of the "Fire".

It is practically certain that Jón Steingrímsson had never seen or read any books on the natural sciences, with a possible exception of some literature on medicine. He did in fact assume the role of a doctor in a country where medical service was not readily available. For this purpose he had received some minimal training from the Surgeon-General of Iceland. In this capacity he became well known, and assisted a great number of people without charge, even when his services involved extensive travel to their sickbeds.

But even though systematic knowledge of volcanic eruptions was lacking in the outside scientific world, considerable experience was at hand in Iceland. Jón Steingrímsson had already witnessed a violent explosive eruption of the Katla volcano in 1755, and this led him to note that the history of earlier eruptions could be deciphered by looking at volcanic ash layers in the soil. The Laki eruption, however, was a completely new type of event, the like of which has not happened since, although a number of lava flows have been studied in detail in the two centuries that have passed. It appears that the present book is based on a detailed diary, where he documents his observations from day to day. It is noteworthy how he succeeds in finding words to describe clearly phenomena no one has ever seen before and give a vivid picture that the modern reader can easily visualise, although some of this linguistic quality is inevitably lost in a translation.

The text includes observations and interpretations which did not become a part of scientific knowledge until much later, some of them not until this century. Thus he performs an experiment and concludes that the temperature of lava is below the melting point of common rock. The practical point was to convince people that, in spite of this terrifying fire, the old mountains would not melt down. He is the first to describe what later became known as Pele's hair, and he gives a detailed description of how flowing lava intrudes surface strata and reappears unexpectedly on the surface away from the tip of the flow.

The most impressive passage and the culmination of the narrative is to be found where he recounts the incident which made him a legendary figure in the minds of Icelanders, the story of that fateful day when the lava threatened to destroy his church. In Jón Steingrímsson's mind there is no question that a "miracle" occurred. He does not want to take any credit because he knows that it was due to God's intervention. It is followed by a moving passage in which the faithful believer struggles with the curious scientist. He simply had to find out how God managed to stop the lava. Exactly two centuries later, in 1973, that method was used by man to stop the lava of the eruption in Heimaey, Iceland.

The reader of this text will soon discover that besides being a dramatic description of a unique natural event it is a sobering account of people and their suffering, when all means of human survival are destroyed and no help is forthcoming from outside. The only assistance available is from God and his humble servant and spokesman, Jón Steingrímsson. Therefore the text appeals equally to people who are interested in the natural sciences and those who enjoy the company of a philosopher with a deep religious belief.

The text includes a large number of Icelandic place names, not all of which are reproduced on the accompanying map. This simplification of details, however, should not detract from the main body of the text. This introduction is partially based on an unpublished article by the late Prof. Sigurður Þórarinsson, who first advocated the idea of having this book translated and published.

Guðmundur E. Sigvaldason

Notes in orthography, pronounciation and names

The Icelandic alphabet includes a number of characters not found in most other European languages:

Ð ð is pronounced like the *th* in the English word *father*. It is called "eð".

Þ þ is not a variety of *p*; it is pronounced like the *th* in the English word *think* and is called "þorn".

Æ æ is pronounced like the *i* in *life*.

Ö ö sounds similar to *i* in *bird* and *shirt*.

An accent over the vowels does not mean they are stressed (stress is always on the first syllable in Icelandic), but that they represent different sounds from the unaccented vowels: **á** sounds like *ow* in the English word *how*, **é** is pronounced like the *ye* in *yes*, **ó** like the *o* in *no*, **ú** like *ou* in *you*, **í** and **ý** are pronounced alike and sound like *ee* in *tree*, while **i** and **y** both sound like *i* in *this*. The letters **au** together sound like the vowel combination in the French *feuille*.

While a limited number of Icelanders have family names, most still follow the ancient tradition of deriving their last name from the first name of their father (in rare instances, of their mother). If a man is called Leifur Eiríksson his name is Leifur and he is Eiríksson (the son of a man called Eiríkur). A woman called Þórdís Haraldsdóttir has the personal name Þórdís and is Haraldsdóttir, i.e. Harald's daughter. Eiríksson and Haraldsdóttir are not really names as such, but patronymics which refer to their fathers. For this reason, Icelanders are almost always addressed by their first names and there is no use of polite forms of address such as Mr or Miss with the patronymic alone. Even with official titles such as President, the first name is used, often with the patronymic.

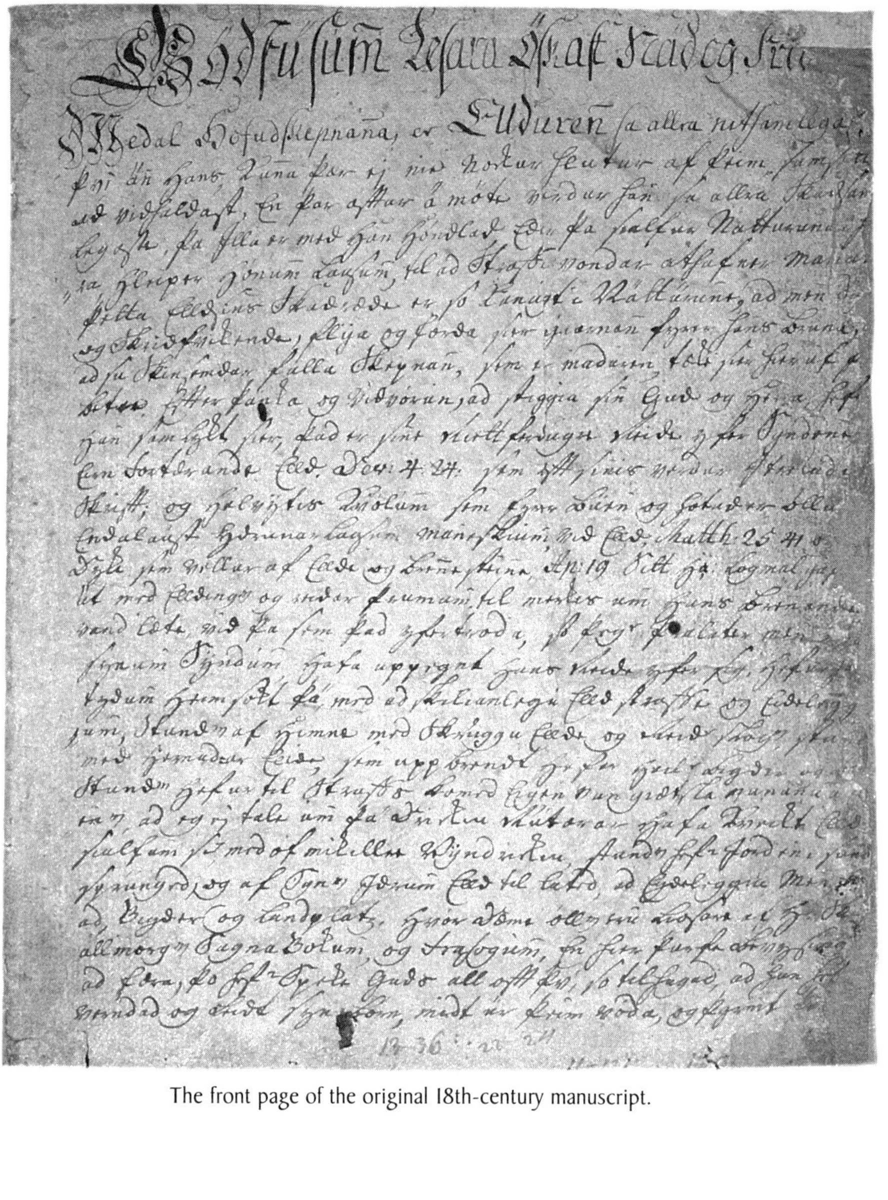

The front page of the original 18th-century manuscript.

Wishing my goodly reader peace and God's blessing!

OF ALL THE PRIME ELEMENTS, FIRE must be the most useful, for without it neither they, nor any form in which they are combined, would prevail. Yet this same fire, conversely, becomes the most destructive of all, if treated uncautiously or if it should please nature's Creator Himself to turn it loose, in order to punish the wrongdoings of men. The destructive power of fire is so well known in Nature that men, animals and reptiles alike flee before it, eager to escape its burns; and in order that his intelligent creature, namely Man, the more closely would reflect upon and be warned against offending the Lord his God, He has likened Himself, i.e. His just anger at Sin, to a fire of destruction (Deut. 4:24 and often repeated in the Holy Scripture) and the tortures of Hell, which await and threaten all forever unrepentant humans, to fire (Matt. 25:41) and to a fiery and sulphurous pit (Acts 19).

His own holy Laws he proclaimed with thunder and lightning, as witness to his burning displeasure with any men who transgress them. And when Man persists in his sin, and draws forth His anger, the Lord has betimes visited upon him the most varied forms of fiery castigation and destruction. This may come, one time, from the heavens in the form of fiery bolts and flashes of lightning; another time as the flame of war, which has consumed whole cities and settlements. Other times the chastisement has come through the very negligence of men themselves regarding fire, not to speak of the drunkards who ignite themselves with their excessive drinking of spirits.

Still other times the earth has cracked asunder, and from its bowels brought forth flames to destroy men, livestock and lands, examples of which are so plain to be seen in the Holy scriptures and many history books and accounts that no reference need be made to them here. Yet God's wisdom has often managed to protect and deliver His children, even in the midst of this danger, showing mercy to those whom it would save and offering them more time for repentance. An obvious example of such have we now experienced.

Both these accounts of the Lord's chastisement and others are set forth, so that men should rather learn to avoid ever again calling forth the destructive fires of God. Thus have our Bishops (by the grace of God) four times had printed and distributed, in 1558, 1617, 1687 and 1749, the story of the destruction of the city of Jerusalem, which occurred mainly with fire and shedding of blood, that it might arouse, as they themselves said, all the thoughtless and unrepentant and strike the fear of God's just anger in their hearts. When God punished that great and populous city, Lisbon, which lies far from here in the Spanish domain, the chastisement caused such pain to the heart of that good and God-fearing king Frederick V (blessed be his memory for all eternity!), though it affected not his lands or kingdom with the exception of the occurrence of several earthquakes and unusual flooding, that he proclaimed a special day of prayer, for repentance and thanksgiving to God, such as was celebrated in Denmark and Norway on May the 14th and in Iceland on October the 22nd of 1756 as witnessed by the hymns, scriptures and prayers which were used for that purpose and are still preserved by many of God's ministers in this country.

Yet now, when this the greatest fiery plague of which men have certain account has fallen over our country, with all its consequences, there was no action of this sort taken either within the country or without, to the best of my knowledge, with the exception of a few ministers, who took it upon themselves to preach warnings and say prayers during the period when this great plague was upon us.

The annals and writings of this country show easily how our just God has many times visited it with volcanic chastisement and other forces of destruction, when He saw that the fear of God and justice had gone astray and would not otherwise be restored, or improved, unless He took control of the flesh. This seems to me to be the case in the district of Vestur-Skaftafellssýsla (Síðusýsla, as it was previously called, according to the Danish Pilgrim and other writings of former times). Within its limits, as those writings show which I have at hand, there have at least 14 times, including this one, been volcanic eruptions which have caused destruction or alterations. The ashes which they have spread have been variously distributed, however, for in some places there are five sandy layers in the ground and eleven in others. The most recent eruptions, in 1783, far exceed any others that we have records of, both in the extent of the destruction caused and the activity itself, in the form of earthquakes which, proceeding in a straight line from the most eastward fissure (but not from Mt. Hekla), occurred in the districts of Árnes- and Rangárvallasýsla, as well as the withering of grass, and an epidemic which caused the death of many a man and animals by the thousands.

Foreign writings show as well that both in Greenland and Denmark at that time there were great portents in the heavens and heavenly bodies as well as on earth. How wondrous the events here were, was even felt in Norway, with poisoning of the air and withering of grass, as is evident from the enlightening New Year's sermon by Johan Nordal Brun in 1786, which the good man had printed at his own expense and sent here to Iceland, without any cost to our church authorities.

Two men have already written of the most recent volcanic eruptions. The former, a Monsieur Sæmundur Magnússon Holm, a student of theology at the University in Copenhagen, [wrote] at the time when the eruptions were still in progress, according to written and oral reports which reached him there, and thus can scarcely be expected to be either definitive or easily understood. The other is the Hon. Magnús Ólafsson Steffensen, newly appointed Lawman designate at the time. He wrote his work on the basis of his own observations, information he was given, and the reports of a number of other men, which he collected during travels here in the summer of 1784. But, as these works are both written in a foreign language, are not in all respects in agreement with each other, as was only to be expected, and have come before the eyes of very few Icelanders, they cannot serve as a warning to as many Icelanders as might be wished, so that they might look upon the castigation of the Lord, which has occurred here, for their own betterment, and I thought it would be unfortunate if these memories should be lost and forgotten upon my departure, as have so many other works of God which have, for lack of care, been lost forever.

The more so do I feel obliged to make known the works of God in His Wisdom, that He as a wall of fire protected me in the midst of this ring and siege of fire, and through all the trials which were visited upon us kept me alive, with an unfearing heart and inexhaustible strength, while this punition lasted – all of which I shall never be able to fathom nor explain. It is thus that I set out to summarize and describe in plain words, all that I had written down, day by day and interval by interval, while the fiery chastisement lasted until God gave relief and brought this plague on our country to a fortunate end.

Everything I now write, according to what I saw or experienced myself, together with the written or oral reports of other trustworthy men, I know before God and my own good conscience to be right and true. Nothing here is exaggerated or overstated, instead there are many small details of the occurrences affecting various households and individuals which have been omitted, as the tale would otherwise have become too monotonous. You see, goodly and righteous reader, that all the arrangement of this work is neither according to the rules on writing and style of some men of this age, nor popular pattern, because it has as its purpose only that which was previously mentioned. For this reason I hope and urge you to value it, interpret it and treat it in the most positive manner; for what others who are sarcastic may have to say about it, or find fault with, I care nothing.

May this, my simple essay on the fires, be thus dedicated first and foremost to the praise and glory of the Lord, who thus revealed His just and merciful will to us and fulfilled his promise, as stated in Psalms 89:32-36, Zeph. 3:12 and many other places. Following that may it be, to my children, neighbours, descendants, good and righteous friends, who have requested me especially to write this, as well as to all my countrymen worthy of honour and love, born and yet unborn, of higher or lower rank, to whose ears or eyes it may reach, for their instruction and education that they may know their Creator's mind and His marvellous works. I recommend, however, as did Þorsteinn Magnússon, who wrote earlier on volcanic fire,[1] that this might serve as a sort of reflection and reminder of the end of the world and the Doomsday fires, which will come upon many unaware, as has been prophesied and which have unfortunately been prefigured here. May it serve us all well in avoiding God's angry fire, so that we may, when the natural warmth and fire of our flesh is extinguished to make way for the all-pervasive cold of death, released from all the fires of lust and evil, cleansed in the fiery oven of temptation, be found in our faith more precious than gold. Thus on the day of the Lord's Revelation, when He shall appear in a fiery flame, the elements burn with supernatural fire, the world stand all aflame, and the damned be cast into eternal fire, shall God lead us into

---

[1] District Administrator Þorsteinn Magnússon (d. 1656) wrote on the Katla glacial burst in 1625.

that shelter of eternal glory, free from the volcanic haze, where we may, together with His chosen (who have been led through fire and water) and all His fiery host, praise and worship Him without ceasing. Such is the whole-hearted wish of God's undeserving, and of all His children duty-bound, servant.

Jón Steingrímsson,
Prestsbakki á Síðu, November 24, 1788

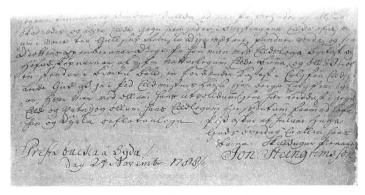

The author's signature, concluding the introductory chapter.

Events and portents prior to the onslaught of the volcanic fire

FOR A NUMBER OF YEARS preceding this volcanic fire and scourge of the land, this country had experienced high fertility and great bounty, with such a blossoming and fruitfulness throughout and the most moderate weather both on land and at sea, but the final year exceeded all bounds. But the disorder and unrepentant carelessness which prevailed here in the district of Vestur-Skaftafellssýsla at this time, in particular in this county of Kirkjubær or Kleifar, is so regrettable to recount that I cannot waste words in describing it. People experienced such surfeit of food and drink that some of them, especially the servants, vagrants and layabouts, had become so choosy about their food that they wished to eat only the best and most savoury of foods. Imbibing of alcohol and indulgence in tobacco increased in like manner, so that during a single year here spirits amounting to the worth of 4,000 fish were consumed at feasts, visits and the like, according to the knowledgeable estimates of myself and others. This reached such heights, that there were some clergymen here who maintained they could not perform religious services in proper fashion and with devotion without the support of spirits; the homes of these same men were later to be devastated, as also befell many others similarly inclined.

Many men hardly knew how many sheep they owned, and even if they did know, the richest of them were never as shameless about tallying up their tithes and short-changed king, church and clergy alike, but it was to no avail for anyone outside their group to find fault with such. There were novel fancies and travelling about, many a vagrant was far too ungrateful, if circumstances were not to his liking or if he failed to get everything he asked for. The prime common pasture of the area fell into disuse and neglect, through lack of order, and there was no organised round-up of animals in the autumn nor related doings, and men suffered losses more than once as a result. Throughout the country it was a general disgrace to see how common thieves had become gentlemen; the law was applied as best it could be bent, and enforced by such toadying, factionalism and acquittals by oaths and lawlessness, that the Hon. Ólafur Stefánsson, Superintendant of the country at the time, in a public proclamation described the leaders of this turmoil as oppressors of the downtrodden, to whose assistance he came by enforcing the law of the land.

All this fracas reached its peak just before the fires broke out and promptly brought the commotion to an end. This fire drove those people, who could scarcely ever remain in the church during the religious service, out of that church and never to return, except those whom the Almighty knew beforehand would sincerely repent their obduracy. The years of bounty which prevailed here led to much visiting by inspectors and ado to increase property rents and fix them for all time, but when this movement had reached its peak it collapsed and nothing came of it, whereby that most just of judges has shown us what His wishes were. Pride goeth before destruction. Yet here I must, with all respect and in truth, except those thoroughly honest persons, of whom there are always a number in amongst the others, here as everywhere else, and who could recognize none of the afore-mentioned in their own behaviour; those men can by their example bear silent witness to the truth of this. Nevertheless, God's patience, and His willingness to wait for men to repent and mend their ways, was so great that He only sent His chastisement when it was long overdue and even then much milder than merited. He caused a number of portents to occur beforehand, as a forewarning to men to exercise proper caution.

I shall name but a few of numerous examples. In the stream Feðgakvísl in the Meðalland area, which was later covered by lava, were seen several years earlier a great number of monsters of various shapes. Near Steinsmýri fireballs lay in heaps like foxfire. A bolt of lightning struck the lambshed on the farm Oddi in Meðalland, killing lambs and splitting one of the supports from end to end, leaving its inner sides blackened as if scorched by red-hot iron. When the farmer was stricken with fear at the incident, and was met with scorn and taunts by one overweening fellow, he answered: "We shall see whether you will be less afraid when your own thundering fire arrives to take the conceit out of you and believe you me, you can expect it." Later, when the volcanic fire descended upon this same man, there was no one less resourceful. At other locations the noise of musical instruments underground and the sound of bells ringing in the air was reported by many reliable people. That same spring the rainstorms had been unusually heavy. Dark red, yellow and black striped flying insects were also seen here, as long and thick around as the end-joint of a full-grown man's thumb.

More lambs and calves were born deformed than usual. One lamb on the farm Hunkubakkar here in the Síða area had the claws of a predatory bird instead of cloven hooves. Horses were more prone than usual to eat waste and scrounge in the dung heap, and even though men knew well enough and had heard before that portents such as these and similar ones generally served as a forewarning of subsequent scourge, no notice was paid to them. And just as God in this way gave various signs to men while they were awake, so also did He speak to many in their sleep, so that they dreamt of events which later came to pass, but would take far too long to recount here. It would also be poorly received by those people who scorn and belittle the value of all dreams.

One dream, however, I cannot resist disclosing – each man judge it as he will – for I know it to be true nonetheless. During the winter preceding the onslaught of the eruptions church services had to be cancelled nine Sundays in a row, despite often excellent weather during the remainder of the week. This caused me great concern, and I decided privately that when such judgment first fell on the house of God itself, it might well bode some great chastisement to come and I was determined to take special care with my sermon. After I had fallen asleep on the Saturday night of the final week in this row, I saw a regal figure approach me who said: "Everything you suspect is true, and it is because you have failed to teach the people properly." His words hurt me deeply and I asked him what it was I should preach. He answered: "Isaiah, Chapter 30. And let it be a sign to you of the truth of my words, that tomorrow you will have a fair opportunity for your service," which, although it had appeared very unlikely, did prove to be the case.

The volcanic fire

AROUND MIDMORN ON WHITSUN, June 8th of 1783, in clear and calm weather, a black haze of sand appeared to the north of the mountains nearest the farms of the Síða area. The cloud was so extensive that in a short time it had spread over the entire Síða area and part of Fljótshverfi as well, and so thick that it caused darkness indoors and coated the earth so that tracks could be seen. The powder which fell to earth looked like the burnt ash from hard coal. A light drizzle, which fell from that black cloud that day over the Skaftártunga region, turned this powder into black, inky liquid. A southeasterly sea breeze drove the dark cloud back inland later that day so that, like other clergymen here, I was able to celebrate the day with religious services under clear skies. The joy of those celebrations was turned to sorrow soon enough. That night strong earthquakes and tremors occurred.

June the 9th was a day of clear weather, during which the cloud quickly rose higher and higher. In the evening a great downpour fell from it. The flow of the river Skaftá, a stream so great that at the ferry site here horses had to swim some seventy fathoms to cross it, and which ran eastward along the Síða area, now began to decrease substantially, however.

On the 10th the skies were heavily clouded, with bitter rain which caused almost unbearable soreness to the eyes or bare skin, as well as a sense of dizziness. Some of the drops made holes in the pigweed leaves upon which it fell, and left scorched marks on the hides of newly shorn sheep. By now the river Skaftá had dried up entirely, except for the water emptying into it from local streams.

A snowstorm, which actually came from the black cloud, blew from the east on the 11th and prevented animals from grazing in many places, as it gave the grass a hard shell not unlike the thickest coverings of frozen sleet in winter. Here the snow covered the earth for almost the entire five days following, and was even deeper to the west in the Skaftártunga region.

On the 12th the weather was clear, with a wind from the south. Now the flood of lava spilled out of the canyon of the River Skaftá and poured forth with frightening speed, crashing, roaring and thundering. When the molten lava ran into wetlands or streams of water the explosions were as loud as if many cannon were fired at one time. At first this fiery flood followed the main course of the river, and then spread over the banks and out over the older lava fields which stretch out on both sides, all the way east to the falls Stapafoss here. (The lava fields which stretches from one end of the region to the other here, from the river Eyjará to the point Landbrotstangi and down across Fljótshverfi, obviously comes from two eruptions, one preceding and one following the settlement of Iceland.)

On the 13th the weather was clear with the wind from the southwest. The thunderings and great roarings now came from some distance to the northwest behind the mountains, with earthquakes and a constant humming and rushing sound, like that of a great waterfall or many bellows being blown at one time, and the noise and rumbling from this direction continued for the next three weeks. The cloud of sand and steam was so great that it could be seen across the country and as far west as the uplands of Gullbringusýsla district. When it could be seen, the sun appeared as a red ball of fire, the moon was as red as blood, and when rays of their light fell upon the earth it took on the same colour.

It was calm on the 14th and the entire area around here was covered by a fall of cinders, with even more of them shaped like threads than in the previous downpour, on the 9th. They were blue-black and shiny, as long and thick around as a seal's hair (it was said that, when examined, they were found to contain an alloy of copper and iron). They formed a continuous blanket over the ground and where they fell on bare patches of sand and gravel and the winds tossed them about, they were twined together to form long hollow rolls. In the evening of this same day a great rain poured down through the dark cloud, even though the wind was from the southeast. It was the colour of bilge, or had a bluish tinge, and was so strongly odorous that people suffering from chest ailments could hardly breathe and nearly lost consciousness. All the migratory birds and other nesting birds fled and the eggs which they left behind were scarcely edible because of their ill odour and sulphurous taste.

Small trout died in the so-called "Fishing Pond" (Veiðikíll) and in many other places. Pipits, wrens and white wagtails appeared for a while to have become disoriented, and whole flocks of them were found dead. Iron turned rust-red, timber lost its colour and turned grey from the downpour of salty and sulphurous rain which fell upon it (the wood kept its natural colour, however, wherever bird droppings had fallen on it, which serves to show how strong is their purgative nature, as doctors have said). The grass, which was green and luscious, now began to fade and wilt; some of it was covered with ash, which men tried either to beat off with a stick or rake up with a hay rake so that the cattle could avail themselves of it. Some people tried mowing the grass and washing it with water, then giving it to the cattle, but it was all in vain unless they still had some older hay to mix with it. That eventually was used up like everything else. The flesh and the milk of the animals dwindled one after the other. Eight pails of milk, holding 20 pints each, were borne home from my milking shed one Saturday and the next only 13 pints. There are hardly words to describe how the sheep just withered away. No one had the foresight to see that it would have been for the best to slaughter them all while they still had flesh on their bones and could be rounded up, and thus have food for ourselves. The horses showed little sign of hardship as yet.

HERE I MUST PAUSE to share with the reader an important account of the divine providence concerning this volcanic outbreak. Great as the threat was which appeared to be upon us, with the surging flow of fire out of the Skaftá canyon during the week described earlier, yet so little became of this fire; as the days passed it lessened until it was hardly more than one-half or one-third of what it had been, as certain observant men pointed out. The reason for this was as follows: according to the reports of elderly people there had in earlier times once been a deep fishing lake between the farms Skaftárdalur and Á, in one of the nooks or crannies between

Nátthagi and Hæll, to the east of the most recent course of the river. During one of its glacial floods the river Skaftá had run into this lake. There were still some signs of sources and springs there.

Into these holes and orfices the flood of fire now ran and flowed, as I myself watched, and four other men who can bear witness to it. An indescribable amount of the fire swirled and churned into this orifice, with splashes, loud whining and spoutings, such as happens when liquids are poured into an empty container with only a single spout or hole. My theory is that the fire, which later began to force its way up out of the ground here and there, came from this source and, namely, that the great spouts of fire and smoke, which erupted from the older lava of Landbrot far from where the new lava made its way, were the result of it, together with the great heat which can still be felt in the stream Feðgakvísl near Steinsmýri. The fire may, however, have run through older trenches, and thus contributed to the heat occurring in places far distant.

From this it can tangibly be seen how knowingly and wondrously the omniscient Lord of All Creation directed the course of events, so that the first threat and mighty advance of fire should not descend too harshly or without warning on any man or his possessions, which they might otherwise have done. Thus, from the first minute to the last did merciful God, having decided to destroy a building or farm, grant each and everyone enough time and opportunity to save his life and possessions, if they had taken heed. I cannot imagine that anyone can be found who is so ungrateful that he would protest against the truth of this.

ON JUNE THE 15TH, which was the festival of the Holy Trinity, the wind was east-southeast. All day long there were great earth tremors and thundering, which continued during the following night. The weather was the same on the 16th. Now a terrible stream of fire poured forth from the Skaftá canyon, so that the entire canyon seemed to be filled with fire. It laid waste and completely destroyed the crown properties Á in the Síða area and Nes in Skaftártunga, both of which were valued at 12 hundreds[1]. In addition the surge of this fire laid waste and covered all the older lava between the Síða and Skaftártunga areas, which was covered with extensive dwarf birch and willow shrub and one of the most serviceable stretches of grazing land. This included the property Brandaland, a productive forest area which had been donated to Kirkjubæjarklaustur[2] in 1350 by Hallgeir Andrésson, then abbot of the monastery at Þykkvabær. It lay to the west-southwest of Skálastapi, fenced off by a tributary of the river Skaftá in the bend it takes when it swings eastward along the Síða area.

The flood of fire laid waste all the so-called yards lying below Skál and Holt but stopped there awhile. A second surge headed south towards the Meðalland area, where there were already two large fields of older lava, Botnahraun and Steinsmýrarhraun. The uproar to the north of the mountains of the Síða area now grew violently, with such sounds of breaking and crashing, fire and smoke, and earthquakes, that no one knew whether the settlements here were in danger or not. Three farmers, who lived at Morðtunga, went to

---

[1] A *hundred* refers to a long hundred, or 120, ells of homespun and was used as a measure of value in Iceland since the settlement of the country.

[2] The suffix -*klaustur* indicates that a monastery (cloister) existed at this site during Catholic times.

espy it up on Kaldbakur, the highest viewpoint in the area, to see what they could of the fire there. There they saw what appeared to be signs that fires had begun in the so-called Úlfarsdalur valley, as they could distinguish 22 large blazes or flames ascending straight upwards from the canyon. When they reported the news to the people of the area many of them grew frightened that this fire would force its way through or between the mountains above the settlements, and I was not without such fears myself.

The weather was quiet on the 16th and I set out on a journey to Skál to check on the church there and those of its possessions which could be removed, and to observe carefully the actions of the advancing fire. While I stayed there I noticed that a dark red fire was erupting here and there in the hollows in the older lava to the east-southeast of the farm itself and far above the new lava-fire (flood of lava), which I approached along with two farmers who lived at Skál at the time. In the path of the stream was a stretch of old lava, under and through which the flood of fire was eating its way, with such rushing sounds, winds and noises under the earth, that it was amazing to hear, and scorching the older lava which burned like woodchips in a coalpit and melted down like copper in a crucible. The outermost layer, or crust, of the older lava that remained behind could be swept off like dross. The older lava, which was thus melted down or dissolved, and mixed with the new stream of fire, turned more brownish-black in colour and became more finely grained when it cooled again, than that which lay under it. This became coarser and more blue in colour (the same characteristics are visible on the trail Lágagarðsvegur on Suðurheiði). We saw that where the flood of fire had not made its way down below the older lava, even if it was porous, it did not set it alight. We threw solid boulders of grey stone into the fire and they failed to melt at all, nor did clay, earth or sand, but was only scorched and turned to pumice after the earthen material in it had been completely burned up. I used this result to reassure and convince the people that our mountains and the necks between them (most of which are of solid stone), were in no danger of destruction by this fire, as people had previously feared, and in time this was proven over and over again, so that this fear disappeared of its own accord.

ON THE 17TH there was a light wind from the north. The flames of the fire then rose so high that from the afore-mentioned canyon Úlfardalsgjá to the northwest, from which a steady rushing and boiling sound could be heard, it reached all the way from Lambatungur, the western end of the mountain Kaldbakur, to the Geirlandshraun, which is a ridge running from east to west, and up in the highlands as far west as Skál. The volcanic fires reached over the Geirland heath, where the Geirland property had a shieling that in recent years one man had been allowed to dwell in due to his honesty. But this past spring two men had got together and moved there, leaving perfectly habitable farms in the settled areas. They were very attached to one another and had more than one common interest. But He who sees the doings of all men and knew their purpose only too well drove with this volcanic fire this comradely pair thence, thus making them the first to leave the area and putting an end to their conspiring, doings and cohabitation.

The 18th was a calm day, with a slight wind from the southeast. Once again a terrible threat approached from the western fissure, whose flood of fire completely filled the Skaftá canyon, which was both broad and deep, with great earthquakes, shaking and steady thundering, [to] the farm Skaftárdalur, which stands on the eastern side at the mouth of the canyon or its end. The farmer who lived there was still on his farm with all his household and possessions and felt it was no longer safe to remain there. As we had always been the best of friends up to this time, he asked me to help him evacuate the farm and I obliged. I got together as many men and horses as I could and set off across the highlands, as now every way below the mountains or to the south of them was completely cut off. I transported him, along with his household, larger animals and everything that could be loaded onto the horses, from there to my own home and put them up for five weeks. But he rewarded me badly for my efforts and the danger to which I subjected myself, as became all too well known.

All that day and night the thunderous crashing was so great that everything shuttered and shook, and the earthquakes made every timber crack again and again. The entire area between Árfjall and the uplands of Skaftártunga appeared as one great conflagration and the fire was still churning in the orifice mentioned earlier. With several companions I went over to the canyon. The flood of fire flowed with the speed of a great river swollen with meltwater on a spring day. In the middle of the flood of fire great cliffs and slabs of rock were swept along, tumbling about like large whales swimming, red-hot and glowing. When they struck something solid in their path or to the side of it, or if two of these great masses struck each other or were crushed together, they cast up such great sparks and bursts of flames hither and thither that it was terrifying to watch.

On both sides the water of rivers and streams, whose paths were blocked, collected to the west and below Hæll and the farm Hvammur, which was soon devastated by the floodwaters. Both these waters, and any others which the fire did not dry up or set alight and were dammed up here and there along the edges of the fire, were turned into a boiling lake or hot springs. From these pools, and the flood of fire itself, rose thick steam and vapours, which were especially foul smelling. Because of these vapours during this week the thundering increased steadily and the downpours which cascaded back to earth tore up and bore off whole patches and slopes of grassy sod, the signs of which will be visible for all time on Árfjall as well as in other spots.

On the 19th the weather was quiet with a light wind from the south which kept the main cloud up north of the mountains towards the glaciers, whence regular crashes of thunder could be heard. In a great shower of sparks the fire now set its course southeastward towards the Meðalland area, following primarily the course of the stream Melkvísl, which previously had flowed from the river Skaftá into a spring-fed river. Near its source the river was called the Botnar stream, for the farm of that name which stood to the west of it a short distance from its source. This stream flowed eastward above Meðalland. To the south, under the edge of the former lava, the farm Hólmar stood on an islet of land, with the church at Hólmasel on a level bank to the south of it.

The farm Efri-Steinsmýri lay to the north, where the river turned to the southeast towards the sea and away from the lava, with the former farmsite there to the east-southeast somewhat farther away and the farm Syðri-Steinsmýri on the other side of the stream. A stream called Feðgakvísl, which began in Meðalland to the east and southeast of Hólmasel, flowed eastwards to join the Steinsmýri stream to the south of Steinsmýri. The farm Efri-Fljótar stood on the north side of this stream and Syðri-Fljótar on the bank to the south of it.

On the 20th the wind came from the southeast, followed by an easterly wind and rain on the 21st. The weather was the same on the 22nd, then on the 23rd and 24th the wind direction was still unchanged, so that during this time the cloud of smoke headed towards the glaciers. The same sounds could be heard coming from that area, the same odours smelled and sights seen as on the 19th. The great flood of fire which poured forth that same day (on the 19th) quickly filled up the course of the river and during the course of these same five days laid waste and destroyed Hólmar, a farm worth 12 hundreds, both of the Fljótar farms, worth 24 hundreds, Hólmasel, 12 hundreds, Botnar, 12 hundreds (although this was somewhat later) and forced so much water towards the farm Hnausar that it was uninhabitable for four years afterwards. It came very close to destroying both the Steinsmýri farms, as the end of the home field of the upper farm was only some 80 fathoms from the fire, and 100 fathoms lay between the fire and the home-field wall of the more southerly farm. The fire did destroy much of their meadows and lyme grass

lands¹. By the 24th the new lava had piled up so high that
when I stood on a cliff, just above the upper farm, Efri-Steinsmýri, and looked westward across it, I could only see the top
of Hafursey, a single peak which stands far away in the waste-
lands of Mýrdalssandur. The same mount can now be seen
almost down to the gravel flats, so extensively has the lava
settled and sunk down since then. When it first melted and
piled up, this new lava, because of the sulphur and salt com-
pounds which it contained, behaved not unlike alum when it
is burnt or water when it swells in freezing and so all the con-
flicting reports describing its height may well have been cor-
rect, as one may have seen it at its greatest swelling and
another after it had sunk down completely.

ON THE AFORE-MENTIONED 22nd of June, the first Sunday after
Trinity, the fine, newly constructed church Hólmskirkja,
which was eight floor-post intervals along each side and
high and wide in proportion, was destroyed by fire. All the
ornaments of the church, its books and burial implements
burned as well, as did the beautiful bell from Þykkvabæjarklaustur weighing 240 pounds, which had been
loaned to the church with the bishop's consent until an
appropriate bell could be obtained. This had been done
and an order had been given for the bell to be returned to
Þykkvabæjarklaustur, but it had not yet been carried out,
with the result that church ornaments and other posses-

---

¹ Ears of wild lyme grass were harvested for human consumption, the grains
dried and even ground and the meal used for porridge or flatbread.
Harvesting and processing of the wild grass was extremely time consuming
and yielded little grain. There was no domestic cultivation of grain for
human consumption in Iceland after the sixteenth century.

sions, which might easily have been removed, burned there and were destroyed. Some people have placed the blame with the minister there who, upon having removed his own belongings and those of others from the church, locked it and left the key in another building before he left on Friday. Another man who, on the following Saturday, reportedly intended to remove the church ornaments was thus unable to do so, even less was he able to force his way into the church to accomplish this, as it was so stoutly built. There is little to be said in this regard except that where God intends to punish the efforts of even superior men are to no avail, as the Scripture says, "Human reason and sensibility become foolishness and poor counsel", as was often shown to be the case in this outburst of volcanic fire, although nowhere as catastrophically as in the case of this minister. He was an imposing figure, who enjoyed good fortune and lived in comfort, to such an extent that he would scarcely have felt anyone else here to be his equal, and many considered him to be a most rational and energetic man in all respects. Now, however, he proved to be one of the least courageous and most quavering of men, so that if his wife and certain of his parishioners had not determinedly taken the initiative of having their possessions and clothing removed to escape the fire, he would reportedly have had little to do with the matter, even though much of it would have been lost, so stricken was he.

The fact that, compared to the others, he was so slow to waken to the danger and remove his property was probably due to a delusion – he had expected the fire to come to a halt and be extinguished in the river which ran above the farm. Both he and others were mistaken here, as it was only natural that the greater natural force should subdue the lesser, as proved to be true here. But in this case it went even farther: as the fire poured and tumbled into the water it was turned into fuel and began itself to combust as if it were the purest of oils, and to this I myself and many others are living witnesses.

Another noteworthy example: the farmer who lived at Botnar, close to the summer pastures of the Meðalland farmers, had seen his fortunes increase greatly in only a few years. When he was preparing to leave the farm he collected together on an island in the river a great number of his sheep, which he intended to have herded away. The fire, however, spread over the river and the island more quickly than he expected, so that after only a brief time there was neither hide nor hair of them to be seen. Easy-gotten gains are some times just as easily lost.

FROM MEÐALLAND I turn my account to the Síða area. As the flow of fire progressed further downwards from the mountains it branched out upon reaching wider lowland areas. As the flow lessened and the fire was extinguished here and there the streams of fire were stopped up and congealed in fields of smooth lava or rough, uneven stretches. Other flows would then follow and pile up on top of them, raising the height of the lava field. When the flood of fire could no longer proceed under, over or through the pile, it was turned back and spread hither and thither outwards from the lava field. The fire had reached, for example, in the first surge, eastward to the Holtsgarðar, which had previously been grass-grown lava hills above the river Skaftá. In its second surge it spread south over Meðalland. But north of these stretches of lava there came a fiery surge up near the mountain Skálarfjall and the slopes and bluffs east of the farm Skál, which stood amongst them in a fair and sheltered valley facing south. A brook flowed down the valley on each side of the farm and the church stood in front of the row of farm buildings. This surge pressed so close against the lower, front extremes of the ridges, that the sod was uprooted and twisted like a ribbon. It is now no more than 30 fathoms from the churchyard to the edge of the lava, which has risen so high there that it is almost on a level with the ridges.

This dammed up the streams and the situation was made worse by the unceasing rain. The inhabitants of the farm deserted the house and fled higher up the slopes behind it, sleeping in outbuildings and tents. They took anything that was of value in the farmhouse and church with them, the church bells, the minister's vestments and altar ornaments, so that they should not meet the same fate as at Hólmasel. Because of the downpour, however, they kept their cows in the cowshed, which proved to be of little help, because the waters rose more quickly than they had expected and flooded church, house and cowshed alike. The farmers had to tear the roof off the cowshed and, with ropes and winches, managed to pull the cows up between the rafters. Because of the blizzards of sleet and other inclement weather which followed they were unable to leave straight away and had to remain there for several more days. The water which flooded the farm bubbled and boiled in the heat. On its surface the farmers and their households, all of whom are men of the truest words in everyone's opinion, saw two dark grey birds swimming. They were slightly larger that the type of ducks known as teals and were most given to diving where the bubbling of the boiling water was the greatest. They were so quick that the farmers could not get within range to shoot them (stories have been heard of such birds in the Reykjahver hot springs of the Ölfus area and in other locations).

On June the 23rd a loud whining was heard from craters to the northwest. On the 24th men from Skaftártunga set out to see what was happening to the north of the settlements. They saw the flow of fire which had reached the river Hellisá in the mountain pastures. On the 24th the wind continued to be from the east and southeast. The eruptions of fire from the crater beyond the mountains were so great that the flames could be seen high up in the air, rising through the cloud of smoke. Depending on the weather occasional debris and sparks fell as far west as Mörk and the mountains Tindafjöll above the Fljótshlíð region and the people of Fljótshlíð and Landeyjar thought that fire had erupted there as well, which proved to be nothing but spatterings from the fires here.

On the 26th the wind was from the southwest and turned northerly that evening. On the 27th the wind was from the west bringing driving rain from the fire. Here in the Síða area we could see the edges or the bottom of a frighteningly large, black sandcloud, which wound its way towards us, whirling and tumbling, up from the western crater. Much of this cloud spread out over the Fljótshverfi area (the more easterly part of the Síða area), spewing sand and chunks of pumice, which never reached this region at any time during the eruption. The farmers could no longer keep their flocks together and the sheep wandered off hither and thither, into all sorts of straits and byways.

THIS SAID WEEK, and the two prior to it, more poison fell from the sky than words can describe: ash, volcanic hairs, rain full of sulphur and saltpetre, all of it mixed with sand. The snouts, nostrils and feet of livestock grazing or walking on the grass turned bright yellow and raw. All water went tepid and light blue in colour and rocks and gravel slides turned grey. All the earth's plants burned, withered and turned grey, one after another, as the fire increased and neared the settlements. The first to wither were those plants which bore leaves, then the sedges were checked, and the horse-tails were the last to go, and would later be the first to return. All of this was caused by the lack of sunshine, clean air and fresh winds, or even the natural dew at night, which was only to be expected after the fiery heat gained the upper hand. The foul smell of the air, bitter as seaweed and reeking of rot for days on end, was such that many people, especially those with chest ailments, could no more than half-fill their lungs of this air, particularly if the sun was no longer in the sky; indeed, it was most astonishing that anyone should live another week. In order that people should not be wiped out too quickly by this pestilence and death, as the all-knowing Lord could see that both myself and others were far too poorly prepared to be called up in haste, in His mercy He sent, in my opinion and from my experience, a cure, for example in the sweet smells which arose from the earth and smothered the foul ones. The home fields emitted an appetising smell of hay, to which the dwarf birch, meadowsweet, wild thyme and each herb added according to its nature, so that anyone who travelled across the barren sands and paid attention to his surroundings noticed the sudden change.

ON THE 29TH, which was the second Sunday after Trinity, the skies were cloudy and the wind from the west. A third surge of fire now came pouring down upon us, so that all the area between Skaftártunga and Árfjall became once more a great blazing conflagration. This flood forced its way into every nook and cranny leading out of the canyon above and to the east of Búland, damaging hay meadows and pastures. It also laid waste to some hay meadows belonging to the farm Svartnúpur (which is a croft of the Búland property) but otherwise hay meadows and pastures were left undamaged. The fire also consumed Litlanes (another of the Búland crofts). The same fiery lava entered the farm Hvammur in Skaftártunga, a crown property worth 12 hundreds; so much water flooded the farmsite that it was never again located at the same place. On its eastern end it laid waste the goodly but neglected charcoal forest of Skaftárdalur and scorched what little woods there were on the hills and hollows to the west of the farm. The fire did no damage to the home field, so that when the population begins to increase once more the farm Skaftárdalur will once more be inhabited. All the charcoal forest of Hæll was scorched but not destroyed by the fire.

On June 30th the weather was fair, with cracks of thunder and earthquakes and a frightening boiling sound in the canyon. The flood of fire streaming from the canyon now split into three separate branches: one flowed west into the stream Landá, which had left the river Skaftá at Skaftártunga and emptied into the river Kúðafljót between Hraun and Leiðvöllur. The other two branches went east, the more southerly of them headed towards the Landbrot region and the more northerly east along the settlements of the Síða mountains. The following chapters tell the details of these three streams and their actions during the following week, together with the actions of the subterranean fire, which had set alight the older lava under the covering of earth and clay which was almost a man's height in depth at Skál and had been borne down from the mountains by the streams, as was evident from the course of one stream, which ran to the east of the farm.

ON JULY THE IST the most northerly branch ran into the old course of the river Skaftá, where much of the first surge was now cooling and hardening, and then out of the channel again in several directions, which I cannot clearly describe even though I watched this happen.

To begin with, I shall describe the subterranean actions of the volcanic fire in the lava fields. On July the 2nd fire broke out from under the lava and set alight the church and buildings on the farm Skál, burning both the church and the well-constructed farmstead to ashes. This privately owned property was in former times valued at 30 hundreds and could reportedly support nine hundreds [i.e. nine x 120] of sheep, if not more, but its assessed worth had been lowered after earlier glacier bursts had damaged the property. But since the mountain pastures remain for the most part undamaged, it would be possible to build one farmstead on a site above the former buildings, when land in the more settled areas becomes scarce. The next farm to the east was Holt, a crown property worth 24 hundreds. East of Skál there were hay meadows up to the foot of the mountain, then came the mouth of a valley called Holtsdalur with a river running through it called Holtsá. The farm Holt stood on the east side of the valley on a bank above the river, while to the south and west of the river were wide expanses of good level land with well-passable trails, reaching west beyond Skál. This pleasant land was called Holtsdælur, and its northern reaches were used as hay meadows, while the southern part was a stopping place for travellers. Here and there small hillocks of older lava protruded upwards, their tops covered with grass but most of them hollow under-neath in former times. One of them was used as a round-up pen for sheep, and could contain about 300 head. This fair and useful land was destroyed in the said week, first by the fires which came from below and then by the others which flowed over it.

I watched the convulsions of the underground fires myself, and others know of them as well. They began with the earth heaving upwards, with a great screaming and noise of wind from its depths, then splitting asunder, ripping and tearing, as if a crazed animal were tearing something apart. Flames and fire soon stretched upwards from each of the afore-mentioned hillocks. Great slabs of rock and greenswards were cast up indescribably high into the air, backwards and forwards, with great crashes, flares of fire, and spouts of sand, smoke and fumes. Oh, how fearsome it was to look upon such tokens and manifestations of God's wrath! The liquid fire poured forth over the land so that everything became mixed together. It dammed up the river Holtsá, so that the valley filled with water, after which it crossed the river bed to burn down the Holt farmstead and continued east along the slopes and dammed up the river Fjarðará, which is now called Fjaðará. This flooded the meadows Heiðarengjar, at the foot of the slopes, with water and sand.

Their farmstead destroyed, the farmers of Holt, with the help of the farmer at Skál, undertook to build a house farther up on the heath. They were unable to remain there, however, because of the smoke and other consequences of the fires and moved away completely, though reluctantly, on the 17th of that same month. One woman lodger stayed in the new house, however, all alone until Christmas, when she went down into the settled areas, as she believed in old superstitions that various things were afoot at that time of year which might make it unpleasant for her, but returned after Christmas was past. Later in the winter she was evicted and moved to the settled areas, but died in the spring as, like others, she lacked satisfactory food. From July 6th to the 12th the fire flowed to fill up the space right up to the mountain, all the way from Skálarstapi to Heiðarháls. The first three days of that week the weather was quiet and a great boiling sound could still be heard from the same canyon.

On the 9th ash fell over all of the Síða area, turning the ground black. The fall of ash continued on the 10th. On the 11th and 12th wind and pouring rain beat down or blew away the ash, so that the ground could be seen once more. When news reached us that no sand had fallen over Meðalland and that livestock could survive there, several farmers from this area and others from farther west went to try to find a place for their flocks. They had little to show for their efforts, however, as when the Lord intends to punish, there is no one who can escape his wrath.

ON JULY THE 13TH the fire headed eastward along the channel of the river Skaftá into the narrow gorge above the so-called Stapafoss waterfall, which was high, with an unceasing, whirling pool. The river had followed this course for several centuries after being driven into the gorge by a glacier burst[1]. From there it followed a deep channel east-northeast along the mountain above Klaustur [i.e. Kirkjubæjarklaustur].

On the 14th the fire flowed down the afore-mentioned Stapafoss and advanced along the channel of the river all that week to Töluhvammur, which is a short way above the rock pillar Systrastapi standing about a quarter-mile upriver from Kirkjubæjarklaustur. The fiery lava piled up so high in this deep channel that the sun could not be seen even at noon from the farm Hunkubakkar. When Sigurður, the overseer of the Klaustur estate, and I carefully inspected it that week, i.e. on the 19th, its bulging dome reached the height of the lower paths over the rock surface used by travellers. This flood of fire had flowed over the buildings at Dalbær, consuming them and much of the home field. I expect that this property, valued at six hundreds, will not likely ever be settled again. Although the fire did not burn down Hunkubakkar, which stood on the bank north of the river, the water which

---

[1] Geologists have now adopted the Icelandic word *hlaup* for a glacial burst.

subsequently streamed north from the lava so eroded the home field there that most of it will be given up and the buildings moved to a less-threatened site, called Smjörtorfa, preparations for which the farmer has already begun.

The farm Hólmur in the Landbrot region, a property belonging to the church at Skál, suffered considerably when the streams which formerly ran to both sides of the farm were dammed up, along with other waters higher up. As a result the farm can now only be reached from one direction, and not at all when the rivers are high. To the north of the river, across from Hólmur, was a croft belonging to Kirkjubæjarklaustur called Laxárnes. It was only occasionally inhabited and was so flooded by water that it will never be inhabited again.

On July 14th, the same day that the fire went over the falls, the fourth and final terrible surge of lava poured forth from the canyon with boiling sounds, cracking and smashing and such quaking underground, as if everything were likely to break apart. This brought on so much thunder and lightning, that scarcely a moment passed between bolts for days on end. Flashes of fire were everywhere around us both indoors and out, but no one was killed outright by them. All week long neither sun nor sky could be seen for the thick clouds of fumes and smoke which blanketed the area. The estate overseer at Kirkjubæjarklaustur, Sigurður Ólafsson, now took all the goods he could move from the church and the cloister to safer places, as it now appeared that the flood of fire would destroy them, so near had it come. The people of Holt and Skál now fled from their refuge up on the heath, as was mentioned previously, on the 17th. Any remaining animals huddled together in small groups, numbed by the terrors which hung over them, or darted about calling piteously; some simply lay down and died in their tracks.

The tumult reached its peak on July 18th, and I imagined nothing but collapse and destruction. I scarcely expect that a single person here in the Síða area could have fallen into a peaceful or secure sleep, such was the night's calm that God provided us with at the time. Everything was then covered with sand, which completely ruined all grazing in the Fljótshverfi region as far as the river Djúpá. All the people who lived west of the river, and had not already fled, now did so, bringing their cows up here to Síða, with the exception of the farmer from Kálfafellskot and one other, who went to Núpstaður for awhile, and from there east into the Öræfi region. No one could take their milking sheep with them, as the animals fled in all directions.

ON JULY 20TH, the fifth Sunday after Trinity, the skies continued to be heavily overcast with the same thunder and lightning, and rumbling and thudding in the earth. But as the weather was quiet, I proceeded to the church, along with all of those people then in the Síða area who could manage to do so, both former residents and newer arrivals. I was filled with sorrow at the thought that this might well be the last service to be held in the church, as the terror which now threatened and approached ever nearer appeared likely to destroy it as it had the other two.

As we approached, the clouds of hot vapours and fog coming from the fire farther down the river channel were so thick that the church could hardly be seen, or its outline could only be hazily seen, from the doors of the cloister building. Claps of thunder were followed by such great flashes of lightning, in series after series, that they lit up the inside of the church and the bells echoed the sound, while the earth tremors continued unabated. Great as was the calamity which had come upon us and threatened us yet further, and taught both me and others to pray to God with proper meekness that He in His mercy should not be so quick to destroy us and this His house – just as great was His almighty strength in our weakness. Both myself and all the others in the church were completely unafraid there inside its walls. No one showed any signs of fleeing or leaving during the service, which I had made slightly longer than usual. Now no length of time spent talking to God could be too long. Each and every person was without fear, asking His mercy and submitting to His will. I have no reason to believe otherwise than that every man was prepared to die there, if this would have pleased Him, and would not have left even if things had become worse, because now it was impossible to see where there was a safe place. Of this I shall say no more, so that it will not be said with truth enough that I wish to seek the praise of men for myself or others. No, not to us, but to Thy name alone, Lord, is the glory due.

Let us look instead at what happened here due to the power of the Lord and according to His will. After the service concluded and men went to see how the fire had advanced, it turned out that it had come not a foot nearer than before. During the time which had elapsed, it had collected and piled up in the same place, layer upon layer, in

49

a downward-sloping channel some 70 fathoms wide and 20 deep, and will rest there in plain sight until the end of the world, unless transformed once again. The rivers Holtsá and Fjaðará poured over the dams which the new lava had made them, and with great torrents and splashing smothered the fire, which was churning and rumbling in the channel, then poured forwards and off the front of the aforementioned pile, streaming and splashing. There was so much water that horses could not cross the river at all by the cloister all that day.

We left the church more cheerful than I can describe and thanked God for the very visible protection and deliverance that He had granted to us and His house. Yes, and may everyone who sees this almighty work and hears of it spoken, whether alive or yet unborn, praise and proclaim His worthy name. From this day onwards the fire did no major damage to my parish in this way.

On the 21st the weather was mild, which it had not been for many days prior to that, and the sun shone for most of the day. The cloud moved to the northwest and from then on no great rumblings or shrieks were heard any longer from the western canyon, although the fires both burned continuously and lava poured forth from it until some time in September.

On the 22nd the sky was scarcely to be seen. Early in the day the wind was from the west, and continued in the same direction on the 23rd. On the 24th there was a great glow of fire everywhere, a downpour fell that evening. On the 25th the same fire glow and wind from the west. On the 26th the weather was quiet, on the 27th wind from the southwest with a great deal of rain and thunder. On the 28th the rain came from the west bringing sand and a strong, foul smell. What newsworthy events took place in the remaining three days of the month will be described later. I now turn my story back in time to tell of the progress of the other two streams of fire which began to pour forth on June the 30th.

THE MORE SOUTHERLY of the two branches, which continued southwards along the former course of the river Skaftá, headed towards Landbrot, where it tumbled about in the old lava fields and hills until it had reached somewhat farther east than the so-called Vaðhella, where it laid waste much of the lyme grass lands which belonged to the Hraun farms of Landbrot. It then headed southeast following the deep channel to the west of Lútandafit and into the large barren bowl to the west and southwest in the land of Efri-Steinsmýri, where there was in former times a lake with very good fishing, which had been destroyed by a glacier burst in the river Skaftá. (There was such good trout fishing in the lake and the river Steinsmýrarfljót that the papist priors here in Kirkjubæjarklaustur demanded that the farmers at Steinsmýri and Fljótar pay them 60 pails of pickled or salted trout, as can be read in Bishop Vilchin's inventory.)

When the fire began to flow in this direction, the Rev. Jón Hjaltalín left his parish of Kálfafell permanently and moved to Hvammur in the valley of Norðurárdalur. Many farmers also fled, finding themselves a place to farm wherever they could, as they still feared that the fire would reach the sea and cut off all travel. Some made no attempt at journeys to fetch provisions, others turned back to their families after having made preparations to go, to wait and see where the fire would end up, and then intending, if it should reach the sea, to flee to the eastern regions. Others set off to transport supplies as near their homes as they could while they still could obtain horses to do so. Because of all of this uncertainty it was decided that the overseer and I should remain at home in the parish, to assist and advise people, whatever should come to pass. As things turned out, however, the Almighty stopped the flow of the fire, leaving a narrow strip between the fire and the impassable pools and marshes, so that travellers could make their way to and fro on necessary errands until the river Eldvatn, which later developed, filled these impassable places with sand. Afterwards, when they had been damaged again, a boat was used to cross the river.

THE MOST WESTERLY of the streams of fire, which followed the course of the river Landá, now laid waste the farm Botnar, valued at 12 hundreds, and burnt up all the farm buildings. At that time the wind was from the east and the fire vapours spread west over the Mýrdal region. Both myself and others who were travelling about that day, noticed the smell of burning wood in Steigarháls, which is about a day's journey away from there. This flood of fire then spread itself out over the land of the farms of Austari-Ásar and Ytri-Ásar, approaching the high land upon which these farms stand. There it laid waste and covered with lava hay meadows, pastures and lyme grass lands belonging to the farms, especially Austari-Ásar. This flood of fire continued on to the

river Kúðafljót, filling up much of its course, and then flowing a good way along it until it stopped some distance
above Leiðvöllur. In so doing it dammed up Tungufljót and
the river Hólmsá at Hrífunes. The whole area, up to the
gravelly knolls of the gorge Fauskalækjargljúfur, was turned
into a fjord, covering the meadows of Flöguengjar as far as
the ford Hemruvað. But when it had reached the point
where it began eroding the meadowlands of Hrífunes on the
eastern and northeastern side it began to subside in the
meadows of Flöguengjar and the surrounding area. On the
12th of this same month the farm Nes in Skaftártunga, valued at 12 hundreds, was completely burned. On the 13th
Rev. Sigurður Högnason held his final service in Ásakirkja
before fleeing finally on the 16th and making arrangements
regarding all the church possessions.

For the rest of this month, throughout August and into
September, the fire ran out of this side of the canyon, then
stopped completely late in September. Goods and sheep
were then transported across the new lava west of the farm
Skaftárdalur, because the fire was still so extensive up in the
mountains that it dried up all the rivers to the north. From
this spot the fire could be seen burning in two locations
until January 14, 1784. Over in the eastern area of
Skaftártunga near the fire the cyclones and lightnings were
much greater than here in the central area. This was likely
also true of the area to the east of the canyon, on the
Skaftárdalur side, as there one can see splashes of rock
which have fallen to the earth. Some of them are long and
wound in a circle, like cow pats, some are whole and others
have been smashed into pieces in falling.

One noteworthy example of such is the following: when the farmer who lived at Hvammur, who was called Bárður Vigfússon, realised that fire and water would destroy that same farm, he had a large chest, containing various carpentry tools and another smaller locked chest of books, taken to a safer place high up on a slope. The chest was later found broken apart, one of its hinges broken, the other pulled out. The smaller chest had been smashed into pieces and the books it contained spread over the ground some distance away. Hay cribs and manure boxes and inch-thick planks were shattered and rent from one end to another. Another chest, containing clothing, wool and brass objects was also found broken, the wool and clothing rent asunder and scattered, and few of the brass objects were to be found. There was also a small chest containing money and it was found a long way off, still in one piece and unopened. My words are based on the report of the man himself to whom this happened, written in his own hand.

ON THE 29TH OF JULY the weather was quiet. It was then that the first thuds and rushing sounds were heard to the northeast of the mountain Kaldbakur, in the direction of a high peak called Blængur stretching up from the mountain pastures. The noises and cracking sounds were no less than they had been in the canyon to the west, which had now subsided. That same day a frightening cloud rose into the sky bringing a shower of sand, most of which fell on the Fljótshverfi region and here in the eastern part of Síða. As a result of the cloud, there was hardly enough daylight to make it possible to work indoors without light.

The weather was mild and quiet on the 30th, and now the thuds, cracking and thundering were all around us, with hardly any pause. On the 31st the cloud of smoke and steam moved along the gorge of the river Hverfisfljót, which was almost as wide and deep as that of the river Skaftá, and contained almost as much water. In some of the channels the water seethed with the heat. I had to make the journey across that day to administer the last rites to a man in Seljaland who was mortally ill, and I had a difficult time making the crossing. The same shrieking continued in this gorge on the 1st, 2nd and 3rd of August, accompanied by quaking, thunder and lightning, with a flow of fire behind the mountains which dried up the river Hverfisfljót. Those of us here in the Síða area took advantage of the opportunity, on the 4th of August, to go to the mouth of the river where it empties into the sea. It now had so little water that a person could wade across it anywhere and we caught 26 seals there.

On August 7th the first visible stream of fire poured forth from the Hverfisfljót gorge. On the 8th and 9th it continued to follow the course of the river, which here on the Síða side lay to the south-southwest far out onto the sand flats, past the hill known as Orustuhóll. The flood of fire was so great that the hill appeared to be submerged, so little of it was to be seen. On the eastern side this surge reached slightly past the point Dalshöfði. This flood of fire continued steadily and piled up, layer upon layer, until the 14th of the month, when it ceased. It had laid waste two farms, which stood upon opposite sides of the channel, Ytri-Dalur and Austari-Dalur, among the best of sheep farms.

THOSE TERRORS THAT FELL over and upon us here in Síða, with one
fire raging to the west of us and another to the north and east,
I can hardly describe. The portals opening outward between
these stretches of burning lava stood at about midmorn, on
the one side, to half-past one on the other and the clear signs
of this will stand until the end of the world. Even this interval
was often filled with smoke and vapours by the force of the
huge cloud. The intolerable reek and odour from the western
canyon was such that from its cloud the smell was as if burning coal had been doused with urine or other acrid substance.
From the eastern canyon the smell was like burning wet weeds
or some such slimy material. All of this mixed together. It will
be for all eternity a source of the greatest wonder, that any living thing should have survived at all here in Síða.

These clouds rose so high that at the zenith there was sel-
dom more than a quarter of the sky to be seen, and sometimes
none of it. When the two clouds came together and the
humours in them became too heavy, a putrid-smelling, sandy
downpour fell from them with lightning accompanied by claps
of thunder, even though the surrounding weather was clear and
fine. Those people who earlier had feared a single clap of thunder were now among the more courageous. I can say as witness
to the omnipotence of God in the face of my frailty that,
despite everything that swept over us, no matter how the sparks
flew and crackled about me, in my heart there was neither fear
nor dread, but instead a new strength and determination not to
flee now, but stand at my post more steadfast than ever so long
as my life and strength should hold out and all the others had
either died or fled, if God should so wish it. And the minister
was thought to have an important role to play.

When the surge of fire subsided somewhat, as it generally did when the moon was new or full, the earth came back to life somewhat, and some people hesitated to send their cows away to regions undamaged by the eruptions. But in the week following that afore-mentioned, when the flood of fire lay on both sides, the air lost its natural warmth and the grass began to wither, both here and in other areas. Now everyone who had not already done so sent their cows and horses south to Meðalland, with the exception of a very few animals, whose lives were allowed to hang in the balance. From August the 11th to June the 25th of the following year I kept no cow in my household, and the same was true of several others.

FROM THE 10TH TO THE 17TH of this same month the weather was as a rule good. The rushing sound continued in the canyon to the east as did the flow of fire from it, so that it threatened to spill over into the Fljótshverfi region. Since the church at Kálfafell and its possessions, along with the farm itself, had to be considered as under my care I had planned to make the journey there to bring back its ornaments, but for many days had had no opportunity of doing so. On August 14th a southwest wind drove the cloud off somewhat. I then went up past Hörgsland, eastward up on the heath, to see whether there was a possibility of crossing over in front of the point where the lava flow had advanced. There I saw a huge flood of water churning seaward to the east of the lava which was simply impossible to cross. At that time the Dalir farms had not yet been completely destroyed and the fire had not reached west of the hill Ey, under which the farm referred to in inventories as Þverárdalur stood before it was laid waste in a snow avalanche. I now saw that the fire was making its way northeast of Eiríksfell, so if it flowed eastward there as in former times, it meant Kálfafell was not safe.

From the 17th to the 23rd the flow of the fire forward slowed considerably, but the rushing sound from the eastern canyon continued unchanged. The small rainshowers were always mixed with sand. The waters previously mentioned now began to subside, as the farmer of Þverá clearly noticed, and he began preparations to leave for good when the fire and water began to damage his home field and hay meadows. On the 20th I decided to make an attempt to journey eastward, but could not manage to find anyone to accompany me, mostly due to fear, except one lad from Hörgsland. When I reached the river Brunná at Hvoll I first sank into quicksand and then had to swim the horse from one bank to the other. I went to look in on the people at Núpsstaður and then to Kálfafell. I took all the church possessions that I could manage to carry with me and returned by the common route which was further inland, thinking the water would be shallower there than at Hvoll, which proved to be the case. But so much glacial silt and floodwater had collected on those alluvial flats that it took the boy and I from six o'clock one evening until around nine the next morning to cross there, and we were almost overcome by exhaustion and wet to the bone. After that no one crossed there. From the 23rd to the 31st the situation continued unchanged, with the exception that a great commotion and cracking sounds began again from the eastern canyon. Thus did this month come to an end.

ON THE IST OF SEPTEMBER a second terrifying surge of fire burst
forth from the eastern canyon, destroying finally and completely all the buildings and fields of Austari- and Ytri-
Dalur. Men who were there at the time witnessed the
destruction. This fire headed eastward along the slopes in
front of Seljaland, covering and destroying all the hay
meadows at the bottom of the slopes which belonged to
that farm. It dammed up the river Brunná just above and
across from Núpar, then followed its course along the older
lava as far as Hvoll, where it stopped short of destroying
the route used by travellers. It was plain to be seen here, as
with the southernmost flow of lava in Meðalland, what the
Lord of nature had intended. The river Brunná later found
a new course following the old lava, much of which it eroded and thus damaged the lamb-pen field at Núpar. All that
week it rained water or brine, with fog and smoke, thunder
and lightning. There was such a mass of fire beyond the
mountains that it dried up and combusted all the lakes and
streams which had previously coursed the gravel flats, so
that I was able to make a completely dry crossing to the
eastern region on the 7th of the month.

On the 10th and 11th a new surge of fire poured forth
from the canyon, tumbling about in the lava which had preceded it. The foul odour accompanying this surge was so
great that none of the remaining animals could profitably
eat the grass for several days. On top of this an east wind
brought a great shower of ash on the 14th of September,
but it reached no farther than the river Geirlandsá. From
the 14th to the 26th of September the advance of the lava
slowed considerably, but as soon as the sky dimmed in the

evening the glow of the fire beyond the mountain was so great that it filled the sky halfway to the top, rising up especially in two locations, seen from here in Prestsbakki. The glow from the western channel filled up the distance between Lambatungur and Kaldbakur, while the eastern channel filled up the distance between Kaldbakur and Vothamar. Whenever the sun or the moon could be seen on that part of the sky where the fire vapours swirled about, each appeared red as blood. The steam and vapours which rose up from the earth here were so unusual that during the entire summer after the fire broke out no rainbow was seen (men call it the bow of peace because of the covenant made by God when he placed it in the sky), whatever direction the sun shone on the clouds and falling rain, until the 21st of September, when it appeared for a long time before the service, as this was a Sunday. However little the rainbow had been valued before, it was now welcomed warmly by many, who in their hour of need gained support from the promise that God would no longer allow either fire or water to destroy the settlement here, which many had previously feared because of the blocked and pent-up waters. Nor were they to be disappointed in their faith and hopes, because from that day on no one suffered severe damage from any flooding. Both the rivers Skaftá and Hverfisfljót and all the streams of the mountains above the settlements have now found themselves a path once more and have not as yet caused any great damage. The two surges of lava yet to come were set such strong and wise limits that they did not manage to hurt us at all.

ON SEPTEMBER 26TH great shaking or earthquakes were felt once more, especially here in the eastern Síða and Fljótshverfi regions. They were followed by some outbursts of great fire beyond the mountains which dried up a great portion of the rivers and streams which had made their way through the lava, so that men crossed at numerous spots, as was previously described near Skaftárdalur. They increased yet again the cloud of smoke and steam from the fire due north of the headland Lómagnúpur and north-northwest of the Öræfi region, which once before had been seen far to the east-northeast of Síða. I sighted it, as did several other men, from these locations. This fiery commotion behind the mountains continued right up until the 24th of the following month of October. From that day onwards there was a great shaking and a strong, foul odour from the east-northeast, which indicated to us that all these natural outbursts had not yet come to an end, as became evident on the 25th of October. A great spout of flame shot upwards into the air from that location accompanied by a terrible surge of fire, with cracking and thudding continuing for a full five days. This flood of fire filled the canyon and all the lowland area between the mountains Eiríksfell and Miklafell here in the backlands of Síða (Kaldbakur is much farther to the west and closer to the settlements here, and there is a long stretch of land and high necks between it and eastward to the canyon). The stream of fire then turned westward at the farm Ytri-Dalur, filling up that valley as far west as Ey, flowed out into the previous new lava, raising it to more than double its previous height inland and to the east of Þverá, as the signs clearly show. It then poured forth between both the new stretches of lava and over the so-called Seljalandsaurar flatlands, which were used as grazing land and hay meadows for three farms, Seljaland, Núpar and Hvoll (since each of these three farms had different tenants and were under different administrators, there were endless complaints, accusations and swearing of oaths, as well as litigation, regarding this property, beginning at least as far back as 1717, which was now, fortunately, brought to an end, as that most just of all judges now showed who was in the right). This surge of fire, which was the final in the series here, was the most threatening and the most powerful. Omniscient and Almighty God directed its flow between the flows of lava which had preceded it and had now cooled and were like stone walls on both sides, preventing it from destroying either the Fljótshverfi region or Síða, which it would otherwise have done. I took this immediately as a sign that He, who created and directed it all, intended to let our settlement here prevail, as came to pass. This final flow of lava is the one which protrudes the farthest to the east of the river Eldvatn and south of the river Hverfisfljót, where it meets the river Brunná to the west-southwest of Hvoll.

On the 2nd of November I held a service at Kálfafell for the people who still remained at Núpstaður and Kálfafellskot. There was a light wind from the north, and so great were the showers of ash and sand which blew down from every ridge, that we could just make out the outlines of the farm and church, even though they stand on high ground, when we arrived on the flats in front of the cowshed (this could be called a day of swirling sands and tribulations). In the evening the wind died down until it was only a gentle sea breeze. The area was one continuous sea of flame from Dalsfjall to the edge of the new lava.

I was to stay the night at Kálfafellskot. The fire cast my shadow as if I were walking in bright moonlight. Furthermore, trustworthy men reported there was almost as much light in the Öræfi region, which lay spread out in the opposite direction a good day's journey away, as the fires reached so high into the air at that time. Here in Síða we set out on a wood-gathering expedition down to the tidal flats, where we had light from this fire to guide us over the difficult patches in the night darkness. But no description can equal the sight.

ALL THE MONTH of November the fire flowed and tumbled, with its glare and flame, through the eastern lava. The strong sand-storms, which the prevailing easterly and southeasterly winds blew against it, did much to slow it down (as sand quickly smothers all fire). Now and again there were great downpours of rain and sand showers, but the earthquakes grew less frequent. On the 24th a strong earthquake was felt in Meðalland, but its effect was much less here closer to the mountains. To the northeast beyond the mountains the fires were so tremendous that the flames could be seen over the peak Kaldbakur.

It was not until early in December that all the flames and glare in the sky began to decrease. They had been visible practically every day, especially at three locations where there were craters or main vents of the fires. But the fire lived on in many parts of the lava, whence it sent spouts of steam gushing upwards. Once the skies were clear, the sun and moon returned to their proper brightness, except when they were viewed through the cloud of smoke. Far into the winter, when the moon sailed through the clouds those surrounding it would appear bright yellow. The bluish colour remained on the ground for some time as well, making the grass exceedingly unhealthy.

On Christmas Eve, December 24th, the weather was perfectly calm and the skies clear. A while before sunset a thick cloud piled up here above the cloister, or above the edge of the slope beyond it, according to all those people who saw and examined it, regardless of from what direction they were looking. It was not unlike a work of sculpture, forming a wreath that was not round but rather oval in shape, like the ones often set on the sterns of ocean ships. The bulge in the middle was light blue, with branches, curls and spheres, extending out into the wreath itself. These were coloured dark red, bright red, black, reddish black, yellow, pink and saffron, with other colours mixed in as well, which I know not the words to describe. A great number of people observed this strange cloud or portent which hung there in the sky without moving, until it disappeared instantaneously just before sunset. Although I can well imagine that it may have been caused by a collection of the various mineral vapours arising from the new lava, which practically surrounded us, it occurred to me as well as others that it might be an indication of the famine and death which was to follow, especially since similar clouds were sighted in two other locations in the country far distant from here that same winter. Whatever men choose to make of this, the event truly occurred. When God acts through nature it is never without purpose. It was thus that this sorrowful era came to an end, with God's help, and a new and different one began with the New Year which followed.

THE YEAR 1784 BEGAN with a spell of milder and calmer weather, so that there was usually a thaw in the air until around mid-January. From then until the end of the month there were sharp frosts and a strong north wind. Foul smells and odours often filled the air all that year whenever the wind came from the direction of the sources of the fire and near-by canyons and occasionally even when there was no wind at all if rain was imminent. Furthermore, the clouds of smoke from the fires both in the settled and mountain areas would begin to stretch out and rise upwards when drizzle or rain was in the offing.

Fire could still be seen in the crater farthest east-north-east. From the vantage point of the cloister here it appeared above the mountain Þverfjall. Residents of the Öræfi region saw it much better, as they were closer to it there. This fire will be discussed later. But after February 7th, in the latter part of the month of Þorri or the 16th week of winter, I neither saw nor heard from any trustworthy men reports of fire having been seen or having flowed from the two canyons from which most of the fire came. These fiery outbursts and terror thus concluded eight months after they began.

Following the strong, piercing frosts and storm winds of January great earthquakes occurred once more, yet of a sort different from the previous ones. Some of them lifted the earth straight up and down again, others crossed the land from the northwest like swells at sea. The frozen ground split apart with no small thudding, cracking and jerking. The most extensive signs of this can be seen in Fljótshverfi. When these tremors ceased, sounds were heard underground throughout much of the Síða area, like a whine in some places, or the growl of a dog in others. Even though I had heard these sorts of sounds described in the Öræfi region when a glacier surged, I had been reluctant to believe the stories, as, under the influence of old superstitions, people believed and said many things like this. Now, when I was attempting to refute these stories for the most part as pure superstition or devilish pranks, I once happened to be out in my storehouse with two other men. Both they and I heard a sound like that of an ox bellowing far in the distance, although we did not expect any to be in the area. We disagreed as to where the bellowing was (or had been), and while we were comparing our views on this there came another howl, much greater and stronger than before. All of us now felt as if it were coming from below, many hundred yards down under the ground, and gradually rising up under the house, its strength ebbing as it came closer until it came to an end just under the floor on which I was standing. The floor itself seemed to quiver or tremble slightly. Now I realised that all these sounds were of natural origin (and were not the crying of the "hidden people"). They were merely the sounds of the wind, of pushing and rearranging in the veins and cracks of the earth after the emptying which had taken place, or of the storms which had recently swept over and blown into the canyons in such great measure. Another example is attested to by all the residents of Hraun in Landbrot. A sound like the trill of a whimbrel was often heard in the buildings there. The people had become accustomed to the sound and were not afraid of it. The farm house stands on a porous hill of lava and when the wind blows into the lava from a certain direction these sounds are heard.

Until this time all water, whether flowing in surface streams or from underground sources, had been scarcely drinkable due to its bad flavour and bitter taste in the mouth. But from now on everyone who was forced to drink it found, and agreed unanimously, that all the water flowing from springs had improved in taste and was even sweet. It was obvious that this was in fact true: those who were sick or even mortally ill could drink water from springs but not at all the surface water in pools or streams. Those men who were not reduced to drinking plain water also agreed on this point.

The five largest clouds of smoke and steam shrank not at all that year. Two of them, rising up from the canyons behind the mountains, were so high that they could easily be seen from the episcopal seat at Skálholt. From there one of them appeared to be to the south of Mt. Hekla and the other to the east and north of it. The thudding sounds could be heard there and numerous travellers agreed that they were heard on the heathlands to the south. Of those located in the lowland areas here, one was below Seljaland in Fljótshverfi, another near Deildarárbotnar above Meðalland and the third at a place known as Þórarinstögl, southwest of Skál. It was this last one which burned the longest, as the amount of soil under the fire was the greatest there. Everywhere that pure and dry humus lay under the fire, or it managed to reach this, it burned it up completely. It was due to the burning earth underneath that the fall of ash from these clouds was often so great, especially from the westernmost of them, whether it rained or snowed. Anyone who is reluctant to believe this should examine the soil and lava in the region of Land and Rangárvellir, where true signs of the same can be seen. All the wetlands were so soaked in poison that no animal would graze there. No animals thrived on what little grass grew there and was harvested that year, and several cows died of it.

Just how great the expanse of the lava was, which fell on our settlement from the mouths of the canyons on both sides, I cannot say. One can, by riding hard, encircle the eastern lava spread in a single day, but I doubt that one could manage to circle the western one. Nor are the lava fields behind the mountains, to judge from the unanimous reports of all who have seen them clearly, any less extensive. They are certainly thicker there, for the fire survived two years longer there than in the lava of the settled areas. All in all, it can be said with certainty that there is no more than a quarter of the former upland pasture area of the Síða region, if it is considered to end at Hellisá, as is traditionally the case, remaining uncovered by hardened lava, pumice and sand, and much of what is left is so badly choked that it is not certain that grass will ever grow there as before.

IN THE WINTER OF THAT SAME YEAR, 1784, there was unusually little water in all the meltwater streams of the glacier Skeiðarárjökull lying between Núpstaður and Skaftafell. Loud, cracking sounds and rumblings were heard in this glacier, until it burst forth into the river Súla, a large stream which runs from the glacier west to join the river Núpsvötn below Súlnatindar (I know of no glacier here bearing the name Súla, only a mountain on the trail north, above Fljótshlíð). This great surge of water poured forth on April 8th, which was Maundy Thursday, pouring first eastwards over all the sandy pools along the western side of the headland Lómagnúpur, into Núpstaðarhvammur and down over all the sand flats to the sea. Much of the water from the burst came into the alluvial sands of the river Skaftá below Skjaldbreið, and was followed by such a strong, putrid odour that it penetrated every home, nook and cranny; we had never experienced such a foul atmosphere. There was also a burst in the river Skeiðará, which drained the same glacier, at about the same time. These deluges reoccurred periodically until about midsummer. Three men were drowned and their bodies never recovered, and two others barely managed to escape with their lives, when they attempted to cross the rivers that summer.

The easternmost cloud rising inland of us was now threateningly black in appearance, but since the wind at this time usually came in off the sea it spread the sand falling from it over the unsettled areas. Only a light sprinkling of ash from it fell upon us twice.

On the 14th and 15th of August that summer, and finally on the 25th, weak earthquakes were felt here which came straight from the easternmost canyon. Since that time we have felt none. The former quakes were also felt in the Rangárvallasýsla and Árnessýsla districts, where they caused great damage to farm houses and buildings, which buckled and collapsed. It was later learned that in Rangárvallasýsla one child had been killed when a house collapsed and two more in Árnessýsla. The suggestion, which I have heard some people make, that this terrible quake began in the Hreppar region, or just east of it, and spread thence southwards, down over the Skeið and Flói areas and from there out to both sides, as this great subterranean storm found room to spread outwards, gives me reason to believe that it originated in our eastern canyon rather than under Mt. Hekla, which I have heard some people mention.

How the other effects of this fire spread over the entire country, causing the withering of the grass and the ensuing famine among men and animals alike, everyone knows from his own locality, and for this reason I make no attempt to record here what I have seen and heard of such. I intend to describe only the effects it had in the county of Kirkjubær, in particular on the land, animals and people during the afore-mentioned two years, and thus turn my story to this.

Consequences

IN ADDITION TO THE PREVIOUSLY mentioned damages to the land, all those useful supplies of angelica root, which had been harvested in the uplands and especially along the canyons, were wiped out after those areas were filled with lava, as were the collecting of mountain lichens and hunting of swans. The last-mentioned was, in any case, more damaging than profitable, because the immoderate killing of the birds by certain ruffians drove the birds to nest elsewhere. The excellent trout fishing which was often to be had here in the rivers Geirlandsá and Hörglandsá also came to an end when the waters of the river Skaftá decreased, except for the little that was caught during the autumn rains. Meadows belonging to the farms Prestsbakki, Breiðabólstaður, Keldunúpur and Hörgsland, which lay along the river, have been turned into barren and sandy lands; most if not all of the islands in the river belonging to the Landbrot farms are now unmowable and many of its other haylands became sandy wastes after the river disappeared. A fine island of sedgegrass, which belonged to the cloister, was choked with sand; a large area of the home field and the buildings of the property are themselves being damaged by the blowing sand, which will become more evident as time passes.

Let us turn next to the situation of men and animals from the time of the outbreak of the fire in 1783 until the end of this year. Both the milking ewes and the other non-milking sheep were quickly scattered hither and thither. From our area and Fljótshverfi they were driven out to Meðalland, Álftaver and Skaftártunga. Some of them met their fates in the rivers, the ocean, the fire, or in the barren sands and impassable places. Some wandered into other farm buildings, and more became the victims of dishonest men than can be told here. Such men were hardly to be envied of their lot, as they were among the first to flee from their homes and most of them died of hunger. Thirteen sheep managed to survive on old hay at Hörgslandskot, two ewes fended for themselves ranging among the farms west of Geirlandsá, and a few sheep lived who were cared for on the Hraun farms. It is impossible to say for certain how many hundred head of sheep died here, as several men did not know how many they had, and furthermore many would have been too ashamed to tell the truth, both before and after, because of their tithes. People slaughtered what sheep they could, especially later in the summer when it became obvious there was no hope of new hay to feed them or possibility for them to fend for themselves over the winter. The sheep were so thin that from 12 older wethers slaughtered here once, only some three pounds of suet were obtained.

It would make for too long a tale to try and describe the flight of farm families back and forth. One sought refuge on a farm which another had only just deserted, as everyone was desperate. Those who did stay harvested what hay they could, obtaining an amount which would be enough perhaps for one or two cows, but full of sand and so befouled that if it were cast on a fire the resulting flames were as blue as if sulphur

were burnt, and the smell was of sulphur as well. Most of the
20 cows which had nominally survived the first winter, though
they had not been given the new hay exclusively to begin with,
died the following year or at least were never the same again.
None of the few remaining horses could have borne either a
man or a body to church as the winter wore on. They died in
such numbers that one Sunday morning, the 9th of November,
20 horses dropped dead in their tracks (some of them while
bearing people then on their way to church) between
Hörgsland and Breiðabólstaður. I made my own fishing boat
available to the people here on the east side of the Síða area,
whenever they needed it to cross the stream below us if they
were intending to come to church.

That summer God provided us with food in the form of
good catches of salmon, which had neither before nor since
run in the waters near the mouth of the river Skaftá; if more
people had turned their efforts to this fishing, it could have
lengthened the lives of more people than in fact benefitted
from it. We in this area were in the worst circumstances of all
this year, as the poison from the fire did not gain a hold on
our neighbours as quickly or harshly. In the neighbouring
areas Álftaver, Skaftártunga and Meðalland the farmers still
enjoyed considerable benefit from the products of their milking animals and some even were able to put stores aside. One
older cow, belonging to one of the farms along the shore with
the poorest of grazing, was slaughtered in the autumn and
gave half a weight [almost 20 kg] of suet, which only shows
how much the juices of the sea can do to counteract pestilence on land. The same is true of the Westman Islands,
where the scourge did not kill a single beast. But as things

turned out the people of these areas lost much of, and some of them all of, their livestock the following year, just as we did, due both to the pestilence and lack of sufficient hay.

THE POISONING EFFECTS of the fires thus affected and killed horses, sheep and cattle; the horses lost all their flesh, the skin began to rot off along the spines of some of them, the hair of the tail and mane rotted and came off if pulled sharply. Hard, swollen lumps appeared at joints, especially the fetlocks. Their heads became swollen and disfigured, and their jaws so weak they could hardly bite off or eat grass, as what little they could chew fell out of their mouths again. Their innards decayed, the bones shrank and lost all marrow. Some of those which had hanks set in their hide soon enough from their head all the way back past the shoulders did manage to survive.

The sheep were affected even more wretchedly. There was hardly a part on them free of swellings, especially their jaws, so large that they protruded from the skin where it lay close to the bone. Large growths appeared on their rib joins at the chest, on their hips and legs, bowing the legs or making them look bowed because the swellings grew on alternating sides. Both bones and gristle were as soft as if they had been chewed. In some of them the lungs, liver and heart bloated, in others they shrank; all the innards were mouldering and flabby, full of sand and worms, and of flesh there were only remnants, as could only be expected. What passed for meat was both foul-smelling and bitter and full of poison, so that many a person died as the result of eating it. People nevertheless tried to dress it, clean it and salt it as best they knew how or could afford to.

Cattle suffered from the same scourge. Large growths appeared on their jaws and shoulders, the legs of some split in two, others sprouted growths, alternating from one side to the other, which both hands could hardly encompass. The same was true of hips and other joints, they were disfigured, grew together and became immovable. Their tail ends fell off, sometimes half, sometimes less. Hooves fell off, some split apart in the middle (it was the first sign of the approaching scourge if the animal became sore-footed). Ribs became disfigured or grew together all along the sides and fell apart in the middle, as they could not bear the weight of the animal when it had to lay on its side. None of the swellings was so hard that it could not easily be chopped up. The animal's hair fell off in patches, the inner parts were soft and flabby, as was described in the case of the sheep, and unusual in many ways. A few cows which were not terribly crippled were saved by giving them to drink of the same milk which had been drawn from them. Noteworthy was the fact that calves, born in this miserable time, had fine marrow in their bones, though little bone sponge, even if marrow had been starved from every bone in the mothers.

Those people who did not have enough older and undiseased supplies of food to last them through these times of pestilence also suffered great pain. Rigdes, growths and bristle appeared on their rib joins, ribs, the backs of their hands, their feet, legs and joints. Their bodies became bloated, the insides of their mouths and their gums swelled and cracked, causing excruciating pains and toothaches. Sinews contracted, especially at the back of the knee, in an illness known as scorbutus, scurvy or dropsy, in its most advanced stage. I know of no instances, here or in any other area, where this pestilential sickness had struck people so badly that their tongues festered away or fell off, unless there is truth in the report I heard of one of my parishioners, who died in the Suðurnes area, but he had previously often suffered from throat illness. The inner functions and organs were affected by feebleness, shortness of breath, rapid heartbeat, excessive urination and lack of control of those parts. This caused diarrhoea, dysentery, worms and sore growths on necks and thighs, and both young and old were especially plagued by loss of hair. This sickness and the deaths it caused were to my mind brought on by the unhealthy air, excessive drinking of water and the unhealthy food, such as the contaminated meat and barley, which those then in charge urged upon people. That men died though they had this barley, one could see and experience personally, while surprisingly enough they survived if they had enough rye.

The fact that the Intendant was so slow with his decrees regarding grain rations from the trading towns for the people here did much to increase the famine and number of deaths here. [Had it come sooner,] less would even have been enough, if it had been used sparingly. Those who did not wait for these instructions did better, and saved the life of many a man, of which there are plenty of examples in the Rangárvallasýsla district. Some people proved to be too helpless and apathetic to seek even this sustenance.

FROM THE TIME the fire broke out until the beginning of the year 1784 the number of deaths its poison had caused was not great.

But from the beginning of that year onwards, as the winter passed the number grew and grew.

Because of the manner of the snowfall that winter bodies could not be drawn to church, and after midwinter there was not a horse left in the Síða area which was capable of bearing them there, with the exception of one animal which I had purchased in the autumn. I lent him to bear many bodies, whether I went along or not. He was an old, stout riding horse, who never failed all that winter, no matter how much contaminated hay he ate, as he got a good deal of grazing along with it. Many a man wondered at his strength and not without cause, but God showed in this as in other things His power and care, by His concern for the bodies of His children. Of the 76 people, who died that year in my parish, there was not one buried without a coffin. On certain days and holidays, depending on the situation, numerous bodies would have collected up; sometimes 6, sometimes 8, sometimes 10, were buried in a single grave. As the famine and the feebleness it caused made people less and less able to hew their way through the frozen ground, everyone who was available to help and could make his way to the church lent a hand in this work. They dug the earth out from under the frozen top layer, placed the coffins side by side and on top of one another, and then placed a good covering of sod over these gravesites, all of which are in the southwest corner of the churchyard. The other areas were unusable because of sand and water. In this single usable section no one had been buried before because of some whim, and it thus was as if it had been set aside and reserved for this use. Because of the lack of horses and men

14 bodies were buried in a walled yard at Hörgsland hospice. Those who died in the Fljótshverfi area were buried in churchyards there. So that it is untrue, although word reached us that elsewhere it had been said, that anyone was buried on farms or out in the open, with the exception of one man, by the name of Vigfús Valdason. He was extremely bad-natured, and cursed practically everything and everyone around him, if the mood was upon him (God will not be mocked). He died of exposure on the barren sands to the east of Eldvatn and was interred in a lava field west of there and a cairn of stones piled over him.

As famine and death oppressed us more and more, people began to flee westward to save their lives, some attempting to find a plot of land somewhere. They had to leave almost all their possessions behind and anything which was not placed in the custody of honest men was ruthlessly consumed or stolen, houses and locked stores broken into, so that it is painful even to think of it. In the shortage of fuel that arose unscrupulous men burned trees, furniture and houses inexcusably, and two farms, Dalbær and Uppsalir, were permanently deserted as a result. Of the 85 farmers who had lived in the county earlier only 21 remained, and of about 613 residents only 93. Of some 50 people who fled from here and found refuge in the Rangárvallasýsla district, only 8 died of the scourge, because the District Administrator there provided them with grain from the trading centre, especially rye, which would have sufficed for each and every one of them if they had followed his counsels. Many of those who went to the coastal areas of the southwest died, because the food they received was too little and most of it barley, with fresh and lean fish in addition. Those who managed to seek refuge with Treasurer Jón in Viðey, the pharmacist Björn of Nes, Rev. Markús, the dean at Garðar, and several other well-off farmers, all survived, if they had not been too badly affected by the sickness already. These men especially are greatly deserving of praise for the way in which they housed, clothed, fed and looked after paupers from here in every way. Of other measures and assistance with those fleeing here I wish to say nothing more, nor of those men here who did not lack means, such as estate overseer Sigurður Ólafsson, hostellier Páll Jónsson, and several others. All of them managed to survive, by doing their utmost, along with the farmers who managed to make their way to the Westman Islands, as merchant Hans Klog does more than many foreigners to help the poor and needy.

I WISH TO SAY little of how those who remained here managed to survive. Four men here, especially, were so well stocked with food, that in the opinion of most men they would have been able to survive even though they received few supplies for two or even three years. They also had money enough to purchase themselves animals comfortably, if they had put it to that use. But in how mercilessly they treated those in need they followed the example of other misers of their sort. There were others who helped out as much as they could, and even themselves suffered need as a result, but survived, as did the others.

All those who knew how, lived as sparely as they could, stretching what food they had, cooked what skins and hide ropes they owned, and restricted themselves to the equivalent of one shoepiece per meal, which was sufficient if soaked in soured milk and spread with fat. It could almost be said that one hide eaten in this fashion was no less sustaining than six quarter-weights [60 pounds] of fish, if not more. Some people took hay, which they cut finely and mixed with meal to make porridge or bread. Any fishbones found on the farm or half-buried in sand on the seashore were collected and cleaned, boiled and crushed in a little milk and eaten as nourishment. Some, although they were very few in my parish, began to eat horsemeat; most of them died. Others would rather die than eat it.

When spring came and plants began to sprout, roots were dug up for food. By far the best and healthiest of them were the caraway roots, plenty of which were found here in Kirkjubæjarklaustur and in Hörgsland, and I would say that, with God's help, they saved the lives of numerous people. Next came silverweed and mountain avens roots, but they were most unhealthy if there was no good milk to accompany them. Both cinquefoil and dandelion leaves, along with moss campions, wherever they could be found, were chopped finely and used in broth together with chickweed, but the sea sandwort was both healthier and more filling. Thyme was also used as food wherever it was found. I remember so well how sincerely many people now recited their table hymns, over foods that they would previously not have so much as considered eating, and it was this which managed to save their lives, more than I can describe. God showed in this as in all else His almighty power.

Because of the fumes in the air, which still remained (and were so thick that, for my own part, I neither could nor

tried to fill my lungs completely with air until I had reached
Álftaver, where it seemed to me as if the fumes cleared up),
and of this food together with the barley many people con-
tacted painful diarrhoea and worms, which had to be
removed with purgatives. Both pigweed and angelica root
were used for this purpose, if there was nothing else to be
had. The intestinal ailments were cured through various
means, some people improved without treatment when they
were given fresh and uncontaminated dairy produce.
Others had to drink well-boiled, curdled milk and whey for
long periods, still others porridge and hard-baked bread of
rye flour and water. Well-boiled sealmeat, without the fat,
or similar remedies cured some. All swellings of the mouth
and gums were cured by warm milk straight from the teat.
Bloated flesh and swollen joints disappeared quickly if
treated with broth made from dandelion leaves, thickened
with meal, as did knotted sinews; to loosen them up needed strong movement and sweat, which was not without
pain, and it helped to have a mercury plaster and sinew
salve of yarrow and roseroot, if foreign plasters were not
available. I found nothing which did more for chest ailments than sulphurwort; tea made from thyme also helped.
To drive out the reek of fumes from the house it was whole-
some to burn bark and juniper wood.

I have written of these easily available medicines, which
God provided us with and came to the good use described
here, so that men would be able to avail themselves of
them, should it please Him to visit our land anew with such
a scourge, from which we would, however, meekly beg to
be spared if that be His will.

ANOTHER LIFE-GIVING source of succour for us were the monies sent
from abroad, donated to support and feed the so-called
"eruption-people" in the two counties here. Just how high the
total sum received was, we were not told. Each man who
stayed on his farm received eight [*rigsdaler*[1]] more or less,
but never more than 16 to those in the greatest need, to purchase animals – cows and horses – a need which this money
could hardly begin to meet. It was, however, better than
nothing to continue to subsist upon. As those who could
possibly sell us livestock were allowed to set their own price,
prices for animals rose and rose, as ever greater numbers in
the country were made destitute by the effects of the fire.
Prices for a cow or horse rose to 8, then 10 and 12 [*rigsdaler*],
or even higher, depending upon how greedy and merciless
was the seller. Eventually one was considered fortunate to get
an animal for even this price. Plenty of livestock was available
in the Rangárvallasýsla district, and it would have been of
much more assistance to us if a different method had been
applied. In Eastern Iceland there was no way of bringing in
livestock because of the impassable routes, as has been mentioned previously. The Superintendant, who at the time was
Lauritz Andreas Thodal, decided to put the money donated,
which was reputed to have been 9000 [*rigsdaler*], towards
the purchase of food supplies, mostly rye and barley flour, of
which people here received only meagre rations, though

[1] The Danish currency *rigsdaler* (cf. the German silver coin *Reichsthaler*),
was the only unit of currency besides the fish. According to a contempo-
rary report from Intendant Stefán Þórarinsson (in the Danish National
Archives, quoted by Gísli Ágúst Gunnlaugsson in the work *Skaftáreldar*, p.
211) normal prices for livestock in Iceland at this time were 7 rigsdaler for
a cow, 1 for a sheep and 8 for a horse.

there was plenty to be had. Because of the shortage of horses many people had to hand back to the men of Rangárvallasýsla half of what they received as payment for fetching it from the Westman Islands or Eyrarbakki. But there was no way of obtaining for this money iron, fishing lines or hemp for making seal nets or fishing nets, which were a question of life or death for people.

God, however, was not oblivious to our plight and this oppression, as that same summer of 1784 a ship stranded in the Meðalland area. There we who could manage to pay for it could purchase a considerable amount of additional flour, hemp, iron, and various other things which were enough to bring us through the worst of the time of dearth and high prices. In most areas here the fall of volcanic ash caused the grass of the home fields and dry meadows to grow fairly well, with the exception of the Fljótshverfi area where the turf had all been burned away, so that there was a sufficient harvest of hay for the few animals there were. The weather was also favourable to taking advantage of it, but men were too hungry to avail themselves of this as they might have done, and exceedingly weak from what they had gone through, some of them still bent and crippled.

This same summer Hans Levetzow, Lord-in-Waiting and later Superintendant of the country, and Magnús Ólafsson Stephensen made a journey here for purposes of inspection, inspected farms and lands and acquired what information they could about the fire and its consequences from those few people who were here at the time, and much of it will unfortunately have been unclear. Later that summer orders were sent here four times for the writing-up of reports on both people and animals, how many of each were dead or alive. These could hardly be expected to make sense or to agree, as people were constantly moving back and forth and some dying. They were perhaps alive one week, and were dead or had moved away the next. This disorganisation finally resulted in total confusion that benefitted no one. But in order that the clear and irrefutable truth should be seen by those who so desire, I include here one census table[1], which shows how many inhabited farms there were and their residents before the outburst of volcanic fire here in the county of Kleif and Kirkjubær, and how many of those same people died here and in other places exclusively because of the effects of the fire and its consequences. I list each individual by name so that no one can truthfully protest against my report. God's wise action can be seen in the fact that He uprooted from here about one-third of the populace and left two-thirds remaining, as in other examples where He punished men by fire. How great the famine and death caused by this volcanic fire were in other areas of the country can be seen in the writings of others.

THE YEAR 1785 BEGAN with a spell of sharp frost, so biting and piercingly cold because of the vapours from the fire which were still in the air, and gave it a bluish haze in clear weather. Once, on the 23rd of January, for instance, a whole pint bottle of communion wine which stood on the altar during the service that day turned to slush. When the clouds of smoke

---

[1] The census table is not included in this edition, but it shows that in the parishes reported on by Jón Steingrímsson about one-third of the populace of 601 persons died in the period 1783-85.

dropped earthwards, the snow fell in heaps, with a crust of ice. Things were quiet in the spring, but late in the spring the sounds of much thundering were heard from the clouds of smoke, loudest on the 4th and the 26th of May, and after that a great glacial burst occurred in the river Núpsvötn. The floods followed the mountainside and one great stream poured past the home field. On the first day of summer and again on the first day of winter water monsters were seen in these waters, which took various forms, large and small. They struggled there against a strong current, certainly 60 fathoms in length, during a good part of the day, while both the residents who came there as well as several clever and trustworthy visitors watched. They were seen once again later, but after the waters had subsided and turned else-where there has been no further trace of them.

How sad it was to see that fertile area Fljótshverfi now laid waste. Foxes made their homes on the deserted farms, as both myself and others saw their lairs, food stores and refuse in a dwelling at Kálfafell and in the doorway of the farmhouse. One vixen gave birth to her kits in the hayshed at Núpstaðir, where she was killed along with her brood by travellers from here and Meðalland. On the 25th of July the river Hverfisfljót first began to run with its former flow along the east side of the lava, then onwards into the easterly bend above what remained of the alluvial plains Seljalandsaurar, and from there emptied into the river Brunná.

That summer the impoverished situation of the few farm-ers remaining here was practically unchanged. All the money which had been donated was supposed to have been exhaust-ed by then. The Superintendant then ordered that all the paupers, who were still alive in the three districts to the west of us and had no one to turn to there, should be forcibly moved here and this was mercilessly carried out. This group turned out to be some 40 people. There were no other possibilities here at the time than simply finding them a place to die, as those who were here already had no possibility of taking them in due to shortage of food. On the 16th of October, which was a Sunday, we prayed openly to God Himself to send us and these wretches relief. We held counsel and decided to head east to the beaches Hverfisfjörur, if God should decide to provide us with seals or anything else edible, and four of us arrived there on the 21st. A single man who was there ahead of us, a farmer from Stapafell called Eiríkur, had on that day, with two boys to help him, clubbed 70 male or adult seals and 120 pups on the beaches of Núpstaðir (though without paying particular attention to boundaries). It was one of the Lord's great works of mercy to deliver so many animals into the hands of a single man and grant him the strength to carry out such a feat, the like of which is scarcely to be found. We had only to load up our horses with the windfall, which amounted to a load for almost 150 horses, besides the butchering portion, which was a goodly amount as well. I then held a service in Kálfafell in the finest weather we experienced during that time where all of us gladly thanked God for His mercy, in so richly providing for us in this barren land and so agreeably removing all the famine and death which otherwise awaited. After this He showed us works of mercy, time and again, to revitalize and restore us. May He be eternally praised and honoured for His harshness and His gentleness.

A great number of farmers and farms here could have been restored more quickly if the money, which was given to them for the purchase of livestock, had not been taken back for the payment of rents and other debts in arrears. The decree of Superintendant Levetzow, which demanded the full payment of any rents owing, as is evident in his own writing of the 19th of August 1786, was not, however, fully implemented.

HOW MANY GOOD and helpful works God's providence revealed to us, during this scourge and after its end, it is and will be for a long time to come impossible to describe. Only a few things have been mentioned or referred to in these writings; I want to mention here several of the things which occurred in the county about which I have written especially. I shall begin with spiritual and religious matters.

Despite how harmful and contaminated the air here suddenly became, He did not visit a single person with sudden death or mortal sickness, which might well have been expected according to the well-deserved and natural course of events. Had this happened, I expect many would have fared badly. It was terrible to listen to the words used by some people, especially the rich, and witness their actions. When they could no longer accomplish whatever they wished all their actions became misguided and they ended by losing everything. This trial did manage to tame them, with the result that they became happier, more humble and more patient the poorer and more impotent they became.

Just as God provided for the physical needs of all, so did He give everyone, whom He had destined and ordained to call to Him in this scourge, enough time for repentance and improvement in matters of the spirit. The 215 who died in this area were in such condition that they were not felt to be too great a loss, with the exception of 12 to 20, according to the subsequent deliberation and reckoning of upright men, and with the exclusion of children, as no one could say what sort of a person they would have become as adults. The worship of God and public church services were restored to a much more respectable and religious order, which still prevails.

On the worldly side, an end came to the shameless so-called "shepherds' rides" and accompanying drunkenness, where each man, with the exception of a few decent men, ate and drank as much as he desired and could afford. It was decided that the Sunday of the 15th week of summer, whatever date it should fall upon, should here be designated for the purpose and called "shepherds' day". It was much the fault of the ministers who were given to toasting their health, that this bad habit persisted. How much better it would be if the custom as it was did not return. The recently imposed tolls on boat or other transport on the river Skaftá, which had never existed before, were removed, and an end was made of the perpetual bickering amongst people going to church on Sundays regarding their transport over the river. Being blocked, the river can easily be crossed on horseback, by churchgoers as by others intending to cross. All the discontent and disagreement that had arisen regarding the alluvial plains Seljalandsaurar and many other matters came to an end and generally remained so from this time on.

This fire and scourge made obsolete the new land registry, which was to take effect here and in many other areas and had been laboured on for some 14 years. According to what was revealed to us of the first draft in 1769 regarding the increase in property rents here on the Kirkjubæjarklaustur estate, the assessment was pushed up to the highest level of ancient times or higher and looked as if it would be a permanent scourge and impoverishment for the tenants if it had come into effect. The first to make the rounds here on this errand was Treasurer Skúli Magnússon, and when his doings proved to be unacceptable for the commoners they fled, one and all, to lay their case before the Intendant of the time, Ólafur Stephensen. The latter obtained a graceful decree from His Royal Majesty to the effect that Lawman Björn Markússon should be dispatched here, at public expense, to re-examine the properties and set such rents on them as he found reasonable according to their condition. With him came Treasurer Skúli once more but, when they could not reach agreement on the matter, two further arbitrators were sent, namely Deputy-Lawman Magnús Ólafsson and District Administrator Jón Jónsson, to survey the area once more and decide upon a reasonable assessment, as there were no wiser men who could be found nearby at this time to do the job. And though men had thought and hoped that they would follow as closely as possible the laws and proper customs in their reports, the message reached us that the distant authorities had not been pleased with the work and that they had afterwards had to provide new explanations and a defence of their work. This was followed by instructions to the District Administrator, in his capacity as estate overseer at Þykkvabæjarklaustur, and to the overseer at Kirkjubæjarklaustur, that each should claim this and that part of the other's lands, beaches, property and rights of usage, for instance, although these had belonged to the property by tradition that had prevailed uninterrupted for more than a century or longer. But just as this was to commence the fire erupted and put a stop to this unsettling course of events. Furthermore, on the exact same day that the assessment using the ancient valuation was adopted and signed in Copenhagen, so that it might apply here from that moment onwards, the earthquakes and outbreak of fire began here in this country, which overturned forever both this and the land registry (regardless of how it was remoulded and set out), both with regard to those 14 farms which were wiped out and still others.

Any changes there were for the better in natural conditions can still hardly be seen. But God's justice is evident in the fact that He destroyed almost completely the common pastures of the area, that grassy-grown and goodly land, that with each passing year was the object of more conceit among men, as a thing of no value or unnecessary for their own sheep, as it had been before. In a similar manner, where there was said to be hate or other inflammable emotion between nearby dwellers and neighbours, there the damage caused by the fire had the greatest effect, in order to drive men from the place and from one another, yet with the greatest mildness and helpfulness. Here the Lord of Nature also revealed to all who wished to avail themselves of it, that there was peat for the burning if they knew how to make use of it, as everyone was always short of fuel. It so happened that, as the fire forced its way forward along the path of the river Skaftá here above the cloister, it tore up so much of the bank along the south shore in the land of Hólmur that it brought to light the best of peat fuel bogs, which no one there or here knew of before. All the mice in this county and the next one to the west, which had often caused great damage to our lyme grass grain and other stores, were killed and there has been no sign of them here since. In the eastern part of the district no mouse has been seen nor made its presence felt for a long period of time, so they may well have been killed off there in like fashion although there are no tales of such.

Consecutive pages from the original, meticulously penned, manuscript.

Ea en Þorun Þorsteina upp biedid til ehss, þvi hún var so rambyggilega vigd
En hvad skal hier til seigia, anadan þad ad sa Guad vill strapt i stigu nidur
mentri flete sin hönd vid seiger, manlog hreinstur og vörsland nidur sa ad vit
læsu og drade, sem vyda aug lysti i Þrætu bledi nodu, þo hvorge so þatsamloge
sem a ehsu byrgte. Hún var hierssona midill og lypte i burtu og mugt
ad nr þa man hönd gala þynt nockur stunda sier hier forn folis og myi
tr, og vary alltid san fan forstandus gta og dugngsta man i olla. En nu
nundt san tyen sa hug minter, gadlaesste og hroddate, ad nema Þona
suns og nidur botnn men hefdu gengust geire fri med sadselgar ad
Roma padan serum fra og satsada undan elldenn mundt hun sasa lytid
skift sig af þvi ad brga, þo mikid frode af þvi þaird, þo vard san sra sier
numin. En ad san tok sig so drent i Dalt sraksi, sma dan ad sleta
syne tygur i burtu. Þsar blaugt sa dalur dregord san, ad ns hos hvend
ad elldurin mundt stansa vid og Holma a Hiotenu sm ns þyer ofan
baen, fa þad Hohonn og Jofnvel flere skel asti, þar d sad ns so nutt
uilret, ad Honn sluta er i natturine sne a san mind ling og sela fords
En his nd var murk ad þeigia; Nutnd a nodan elldurn nr ad salla og vona
i slad vard ad elldo nrtt, og logade sialst, sm tdrasta dst ndr. þsar
til seig og mang nrn ag ter srum ad lysfande troner tit nunn
anad doma ysterstilte nundt, donde sa tr vid i bottn slar nörd
A frett nedallendinga, gieddve slar ntl sir a sanin an nr sla san nr ad
slutsa sig i burt u, samanyagnads san nicklu af sier syne i sun byd
ma i sliotenu hr sia daen sm san dtlade ad vintzta, En elldurin
sliod skiotasa in sair hugde ner tzested og holmanso a lytillur stunda hs
ti af þvi, fölld nir hier; hvad asti sliott syst u stundz og so sliott.

§ 7.

Nu vykt og Toguns þru nedallundenu til syduns ystter sig, sm bled
ins tod zott ad usan, knysladst, þad sa sram a vidi og uydlindar slast
volu gdi: sstter sig; sm þad myntade og duilnade fra og þar, skysladst bram
sra buen ir sunu saman i þell ur þraun og þhungur, konu so adtar
stonsti þar usan a asi sm sorsorsadu myounnd, og thlodu þru usan
a anad; þa elldhlodd tonst ej thengur under ysser bor gurgunar, þan
svnla